Low-Fat Stir Fry Cookbook

From the Editors of Sunset Books

Sunset Publishing Corporation • Menlo Park, California

Sunset
BOOKS

President & Publisher:
Susan J. Maruyama

Director, Finance & Business Affairs:
Gary Loebner

Director, Manufacturing & Sales Service:
Lorinda Reichert

Director, Sales & Marketing:
Richard A. Smeby

Marketing & Creative Services Manager:
Guy C. Joy

Editorial Director:
Kenneth Winchester

Executive Editor:
Bob Doyle

Coordinating Editor:
Linda J. Selden

Research & Text:
Karyn I. Lipman

Copy Editor:
Rebecca La Brum

Contributing Editor:
Sue Brownlee

Design:
Susan Sempere

Illustrations:
Dick Cole

Dietary Consultant:
Patricia Kearney, R.D.
Stanford University Hospital

Photo Stylist:
Sandra Griswold

Food Stylist:
Heidi Gintner

Photographers:
Allan Rosenberg; Norman A. Plate: 3

•

SUNSET PUBLISHING CORPORATION

Chairman:
Jim Nelson

President/Chief Executive Officer:
Robin Wolaner

Chief Financial Officer:
James E. Mitchell

Publisher:
Stephen J. Seabolt

Circulation Director:
Robert I. Gursha

Editor, Sunset Magazine:
William R. Marken

Senior Editor (Food & Entertaining):
Jerry Anne Di Vecchio

First printing April 1995
Copyright © 1995
Sunset Publishing Corporation,
Menlo Park, CA 94025.
First edition. All rights reserved, including the right
of reproduction in whole or in
part in any form.

ISBN 0-376-02476-3. Library of Congress
Catalog Card Number: 94-069952.
Printed in the United States.

Front Cover: For an unusual meal with
Mexican flair, try colorful Veal with Apricot
Salsa. You'll find the recipe on page 71.

Low-fat Stir Fry Cooking: Fast, Flavorful & Healthy!

••

*A*re you looking for light, great-tasting meals that are quick to cook? Do you enjoy sampling dishes from a variety of cuisines? If the answer to these questions is yes, then low-fat stir-frying is for you. It's a speedy technique that adapts effortlessly to dishes of many ethnic styles, from Chinese to Indian, Mexican to Mediterranean. And for fresh, vivid flavors and colors, stir-frying can't be beat.

•

Ranging from warm salads to elegant entrées to delicious desserts, today's low-fat stir-fries are based on the best lean ingredients and enlivened with creative combinations of spices, herbs, and condiments. Among the surprises you'll find in these pages are Stir-fried Cannellini Cassoulet, Couscous Bean Paella, Curried Lamb with Grape Chutney, and even sweet treats like Cherry & Apple Jubilee.

•

All our recipes have been developed to conform to the American Heart Association recommendations for fat intake; in each, fat provides no more than 30% of the calories.

•

For our recipes, we provide a nutritional analysis (see page 5) prepared by Hill Nutrition Associates, Inc., of Florida. We are grateful to Lynne Hill, R. D., for her advice and expertise.

•

All of the recipes in this book were developed and tested in the Sunset Test Kitchens. If you have comments or suggestions, please let us hear from you. Write us at:

**Sunset Books/Cookbook Editorial
80 Willow Road
Menlo Park, CA 94025**

If you would like to order additional copies of any of our books, call us at (800) 634-3095 or check with your local bookstore.

•

Contents

Special Features

A feast of appetizing color, Linguine with Yellow Tomatoes (page 24) shows off the season's best produce. Ripe, juicy cherry tomatoes, fresh basil, and Hot Chili Oil (page 69) give the dish its memorable flavor.

Introduction

∙∙

When you think of stir-frying, you probably think of Chinese-style dishes quick-cooked in a wok. You think of bright colors, crisp textures, and fresh flavors. And you're likely to think of lean, healthful eating: in the minds of many, "stir-fried" has come to be virtually synonymous with "low-fat."

What's the real story? It's true that stir-fries can't be bettered for their colorful good looks and lively, fresh flavors and textures. But these dishes aren't necessarily Chinese: as this book will show you, the stir-fry technique is wonderfully versatile. The same method used to prepare Asian favorites such as kung pao chicken and sweet and sour pork can, with a simple switch of ingredients and seasonings, produce Mexican-style fajitas, Italian pasta sauces, and Indian curries.

Likewise, stir-fries needn't be made in a wok. If you have one, well and good—but if you don't, you'll find that a wide nonstick frying pan does the job beautifully.

Finally, though stir-fries certainly lend themselves to lean cooking—our recipes are proof of that—they are by no means automatically low in fat. If you use a generous amount of oil, if you don't trim the fat from meats, if you stir-fry in thick batters or favor lavish use of high-fat extras like peanuts or cashews, your stir-fry will not be lean.

So how do you stir-fry the low-fat way? It's simple, really: use a nonstick frying pan or wok, the very best lean ingredients, and the very least amount of oil. The recipes in these pages will teach you how.

Stir-frying... and low-fat stir-frying

What is stir-frying? As the name implies, it involves sautéing—frying—with almost constant stirring and tossing. This quick stirring and turning cooks foods rapidly on all sides, sealing in flavors and juices. And because the ingredients are typically cut into bite-size pieces, stir-frying is very fast; everything cooks in just a few minutes. Classic stir-frying is done over high heat, the better to seal the surfaces of each food instantly. Usually, the empty pan is heated; then the oil is added. Once the oil is hot, the foods to be cooked go into the pan.

Our low-fat stir-frying method uses the same stir-and-toss mechanics as the traditional approach, though you'll sometimes be directed to stir-fry "gently." This instruction applies when you're cooking batter-coated foods, fragile ones such as cubed tofu or thin strips of fish, or softer ingredients like canned beans. In any of these cases, wielding your spoon or spatula with the usual vigor could mash the food or cause it to fall apart. When you stir-fry gently, turn the foods quickly to cook all sides, as usual—but do so with a little extra care.

Of course, there are some differences between low-fat and traditional stir-frying. First, we use a bare minimum of fat—or sometimes none at all. Numerous recipes simply replace the fat with a little water; the liquid is fat-free, but keeps foods from sticking and aids in browning, too.

A second, more important distinction between the classic and low-fat techniques lies in the cooking temperature. To keep the oil to a minimal amount, we use nonstick pans—and that means we never heat the pan before adding fat, nor do we cook over high heat. Doing either of these can damage nonstick coatings. Don't expect our stir-fried foods to form the browned, almost charred crust you'll encounter in restaurant stir-fries: for that, you need intensely high heat and, often, lots of oil.

More on equipment

We've noted that a nonstick pan is best for low-fat stir-frying—but what kind should you choose? Though nonstick woks are available, we've found that a wide (at least 12-inch) nonstick frying pan with a tight-fitting lid gives excellent results. In general, you'll need to use wood or nylon utensils to avoid scratching the pan's surface, though some newer pans have reinforced, textured coatings that are unaffected by metal cooking tools.

As noted above, many manufacturers of nonstick equipment recommend avoiding high-heat cooking, and this is the advice we've followed in our recipes. Do remember, though, that nonstick coatings will not perform flawlessly forever. Even with the best care, a pan's releasing ability naturally diminishes over time. When you find that foods are beginning to stick, think about investing in new equipment.

Of course, equipment and technique alone don't make a dish low-fat: that depends on the ingredients you use.

Ingredients for low-fat stir-frying

Like any kind of low-fat cooking, low-fat stir-frying depends on low-fat ingredients and lively seasonings.

• **Choose naturally lean poultry and seafood;** buy the leanest cuts of red meats and trim away all visible fat.

• **Use plenty of fresh vegetables and fruits.** For stir-fries, it's crucial to select the freshest, prettiest produce you can find: the cooking is so brief and the sauces so light that you can't hide substandard ingredients. That elderly zucchini and worn-out, wrinkled bell pepper will look just as tired coming out of the pan as they did going in.

• **When using dairy products such as milk, yogurt, and sour cream, opt for the nonfat, low-fat, and reduced-fat choices** so readily available today. Among cheeses, you can also use modest quantities of whole-milk types such as feta, blue, extra-sharp Cheddar, and Parmesan; these are all so robust that even a small amount makes a significant contribution to a recipe's flavor.

• **If you're looking to cut sodium as well as fat, use reduced-sodium broth and soy sauce,** as we do.

• **You can cut the percentage of calories from fat in any stir-fry by including a healthy helping of rice or pasta** in each serving. Mild-flavored and rich in complex carbohydrates, these filling foods are perfect partners for saucy, spicy combinations of meats and vegetables. Many stir-fries are also delicious with tortillas or pita bread.

• **To make up for the flavor traditionally contributed by fat, turn to extra seasonings.** Aromatic herbs and spices, zesty vinegars such as raspberry and balsamic, and intensely flavored condiments like hoisin sauce and chili paste all add excitement—but little or no fat—to lean dishes. You might try cooking with small amounts of herb- or spice-infused oils, as well; see pages 68 and 69.

When you use our recipes, keep in mind that you can substitute higher-fat or higher-sodium versions of any of the products we call for. If you prefer reduced-fat sour cream to the nonfat version, or if regular soy sauce tastes better to you than the reduced-sodium type, use what you like. Just remember that such substitutions will boost the fat and sodium content of the finished dish.

Another point to remember is that "low-fat" does not mean "low-calorie." If you're trying to lose weight on a calorie-controlled diet, be aware of your daily limit and select your foods accordingly. Many of the recipes in this book will fit right into your plan, but some are high enough in calories to qualify as every-now-and-then treats.

Tips for successful stir-frying

You have the right equipment and all the best lean ingredients; you know the stir-frying technique. What else can you do to make your stir-fries a success?

First, complete all your preparation in advance. Rinse and cut vegetables and fruits; cut up meats; assemble cooking sauces; organize any garnishes; and select any condiments you want to serve at the table. Once you start to stir-fry, you won't have time to stop and stir up a sauce or slice an onion. Remember: to guarantee even cooking, be sure to slice ingredients into small, uniform pieces, according to the recipe's directions.

Second, set up a work station near the stove top. Have your ingredients, cooking utensils, pot holders, a timer, and any serving dishes on hand before you start to cook.

Third, don't overcrowd the pan: cook no more than 4 to 5 cups of food in a 12-inch pan at one time. If you need more servings than you can cook at once, just prepare the dish in two or more batches; you can keep the first portions warm while you cook the rest.

Fourth, once you've begun to cook, never walk away from the stove. Stir-frying is so fast that foods can scorch or burn very quickly.

Remember that the preparation and cooking times given in our recipes are guides, not absolutes. Actual times will vary, depending on your level of expertise, the freshness and size of the vegetables you use, the type of cookware you have, and the heat source.

A Word about Our Nutritional Data

For our recipes, we provide a nutritional analysis stating calorie count; percentage of calories from fat; grams of protein, carbohydrates, total fat, and saturated fat; and milligrams of cholesterol and sodium. Generally, the analysis applies to a single serving, based on the number of servings given for each recipe and the amount of each ingredient. If a range is given for the number of servings and/or the amount of an ingredient, the analysis is based on the average of the figures given.

The nutritional analysis does not include optional ingredients or those for which no specific amount is stated. If an ingredient is listed with a substitution, the information was calculated using the first choice.

Side Dishes

Tender-crisp vegetables, fresh fruits, mellow beans, and savory pasta and rice dishes all deliver welcome diversity to low-fat meals. You'll find that the choices in this chapter really perk up your dinner plate—especially when the entrée is a simple one.

....

Mild, creamy white beans contrast deliciously with deep emerald, slightly bitter greens in Sautéed Kale with Cannellini (recipe on page 8).

Stir-fried Cannellini Cassoulet

Preparation time: About 30 minutes
Cooking time: About 30 minutes

•

Traditional cassoulet is a hearty, slow-baked French dish of white beans and various meats—duck or goose, sausages, pork, and/or lamb shanks, depending on regional preferences. Here, we've elevated the nutrient-rich beans to the starring role and reduced the meat to a few slices of bacon—without compromising the flavor. Seasoned with herbs and topped with crisp, garlicky crumbs, the dish is delicious with chicken or lamb.

> Garlic Crumbs (recipe follows)
>
> 4 slices bacon, coarsely chopped
>
> 1 large onion, chopped
>
> 2 cans (about 15 oz./430 g *each*) cannellini (white kidney beans)
>
> 1 can (about 8 oz./230 g) tomato sauce
>
> About ½ cup (120 ml) Beaujolais nouveau or dry white wine, or to taste
>
> 3 tablespoons (45 ml) molasses
>
> 1½ teaspoons *each* dry mustard and Worcestershire
>
> 1½ teaspoons chopped fresh thyme or ½ teaspoon dried thyme
>
> ¾ teaspoon chopped fresh rosemary or ¼ teaspoon dried rosemary
>
> ¼ teaspoon pepper
>
> 1 large tomato (about 8 oz./230 g), chopped and drained well
>
> ¼ cup (15 g) chopped parsley
>
> Thyme or rosemary sprigs

Prepare Garlic Crumbs; set aside.

In a wide nonstick frying pan or wok, stir-fry bacon and onion over medium-high heat until browned bits form on pan bottom and onion is soft (about 5 minutes). Add water, 1 tablespoon (15 ml) at a time, if pan appears dry. Spoon off and discard any drippings.

Drain beans, reserving ¼ cup (60 ml) of the liquid. To pan, add beans and reserved liquid. Then stir in tomato sauce, ¼ cup (60 ml) of the wine, molasses, mustard,

Worcestershire, chopped thyme, chopped rosemary, and pepper. Bring to a boil. Then reduce heat and boil gently, stirring occasionally, until almost all liquid has evaporated (about 15 minutes); as liquid cooks down, stir more frequently to prevent scorching. Remove from heat and stir in tomato and about ¼ cup (60 ml) more wine.

Transfer bean mixture to a shallow serving bowl. Stir parsley into Garlic Crumbs; sprinkle crumb mixture over beans. Garnish with thyme sprigs. Makes 6 servings.

Garlic Crumbs. Tear 2 slices (about 2 oz./55 g *total*) **sourdough sandwich bread** into pieces. Whirl in a blender or food processor to make fine crumbs. In a wide nonstick frying pan or wok, combine crumbs, 1 tablespoon (15 ml) **water,** 1 teaspoon **olive oil,** and 2 cloves **garlic,** minced or pressed. Stir-fry over medium heat until crumbs are crisp and golden (about 8 minutes); remove from pan and set aside. If made ahead, let cool; then cover airtight and store at room temperature until next day.

Per serving: 276 calories (25% calories from fat), 11 g protein, 39 g carbohydrates, 7 g total fat (2 g saturated fat), 7 mg cholesterol, 733 mg sodium

Sautéed Kale with Cannellini

Pictured on page 6
Preparation time: About 10 minutes
Cooking time: About 20 minutes

•

Beautiful, ruffly, bursting with vitamins—once it catches your eye in the produce department, kale can be impossible to resist. But what can you do with it once you've brought it home? We suggest stir-frying the sliced leaves in a small amount of bacon drippings, then serving them with mild cannellini beans to make a robust side dish.

> 1¼ pounds (565 g) kale
>
> 4 slices bacon, chopped
>
> 2 large onions, thinly sliced
>
> 2 cans (about 15 oz./430 g *each*) cannellini (white kidney beans), drained and rinsed
>
> Salt and pepper

Remove and discard tough stems from kale; then rinse kale, drain, and cut crosswise into ½-inch (1-cm) strips. Set aside.

In a wide nonstick frying pan or wok, stir-fry bacon over medium-high heat until crisp (about 3 minutes). Remove from pan with a slotted spoon and set aside. Add onions to drippings in pan and stir-fry until soft (about 5 minutes). Add kale and stir-fry until wilted and bright green (3 to 4 minutes). Transfer to a platter and keep warm.

Add beans to pan, reduce heat to medium-low, and stir until heated through (about 4 minutes). Spoon beans over kale; sprinkle beans and kale with bacon. Season to taste with salt and pepper. Makes 6 servings.

Per serving: 189 calories (19% calories from fat), 11 g protein, 28 g carbohydrates, 4 g total fat (1 g saturated fat), 4 mg cholesterol, 276 mg sodium

Almond & Zucchini Stir-fry

Preparation time: About 10 minutes
Cooking time: About 25 minutes

•

If you have a vegetable garden, you probably plant zucchini. And if you plant zucchini, there's a time—usually at the height of summer—when you're longing for new ways to serve this prolific squash. Here's one delicious choice: a satisfying combination of rice and julienned zucchini, seasoned with soy and topped with almonds.

1 cup (185 g) long-grain white rice

½ cup (60 g) slivered almonds

6 large zucchini (about 2 lbs./905 g *total*), cut into ¼- by 2-inch (6-mm by 5-cm) sticks

2 cloves garlic, minced or pressed
   About 2 tablespoons (30 ml) reduced-sodium soy sauce

In a 3- to 4-quart (2.8- to 3.8-liter) pan, bring 2 cups (470 ml) water to a boil over high heat; stir in rice. Reduce heat, cover, and simmer until liquid has been absorbed and rice is tender to bite (about 20 minutes).

Meanwhile, in a wide nonstick frying pan or wok, stir almonds over medium heat until golden (4 to 5 minutes). Pour out of pan and set aside. To pan, add zucchini, garlic, and 2 tablespoons (30 ml) water. Increase heat to medium-high; stir-fry until zucchini is tender-crisp to bite and liquid has evaporated (about 9 minutes). Add 2 tablespoons (30 ml) of the soy sauce; mix gently.

To serve, spoon rice into a bowl and pour zucchini over it; sprinkle with almonds. Offer more soy sauce to add to taste. Makes 6 servings.

Per serving: 205 calories (27% calories from fat), 7 g protein, 32 g carbohydrates, 6 g total fat (0.6 g saturated fat), 0 mg cholesterol, 207 mg sodium

Zucchini & Carrot Sauté

Preparation time: About 10 minutes
Cooking time: About 10 minutes

•

To add interest to familiar vegetables, try using unexpected seasonings. Here, we've spiced up slivered carrots and zucchini with chili powder and aromatic cumin and mustard seeds.

1 small onion, thinly sliced

2 teaspoons chili powder

1 teaspoon *each* cumin seeds and mustard seeds

1 large carrot (about 6 oz./170 g), cut into matchstick strips

1¼ pounds (565 g) zucchini, cut into matchstick strips
   Salt and pepper

In a wide nonstick frying pan or wok, combine onion and 3 tablespoons (45 ml) water. Stir-fry over medium-high heat until onion is soft (about 5 minutes). Stir in chili powder, cumin seeds, and mustard seeds.

Add carrot and zucchini to pan; stir-fry until carrot is tender-crisp to bite (about 5 minutes). Season to taste with salt and pepper. Makes 6 servings.

Per serving: 39 calories (12% calories from fat), 2 g protein, 8 g carbohydrates, 0.6 g total fat (0 g saturated fat), 0 mg cholesterol, 22 mg sodium

Asparagus Sauté

Preparation time: About 15 minutes
Cooking time: About 10 minutes

•

Juicy mandarin oranges add a sweet and surprising accent to this springtime special.

- 1½   pounds (680 g) asparagus
- 2   teaspoons olive oil
- 8   ounces (230 g) mushrooms, thinly sliced
- 1   clove garlic, minced or pressed
- ⅓   cup (80 ml) dry white wine
- 1   tablespoon grated orange peel
- ⅛   teaspoon crushed red pepper flakes
- ¼   teaspoon dried tarragon
- ½   cup (75 g) drained canned mandarin oranges or fresh orange segments

Snap off and discard tough ends of asparagus. Cut spears into 1-inch (2.5-cm) slanting slices.

Heat oil in a wide nonstick frying pan or wok over medium-high heat. When oil is hot, add asparagus, mushrooms, and garlic; stir-fry until asparagus is hot and bright green (about 3 minutes).

Add wine, orange peel, red pepper flakes, and tarragon. Cover and cook until asparagus is just tender-crisp to bite (about 3 minutes). Uncover and continue to cook until liquid has evaporated (1 to 2 more minutes). Stir in oranges. Makes 4 servings.

Per serving: 90 calories (27% calories from fat), 4 g protein, 12 g carbohydrates, 3 g total fat (0.4 g saturated fat), 0 mg cholesterol, 7 mg sodium

Mediterranean Squash

Pictured on facing page
Preparation time: About 25 minutes
Cooking time: About 20 minutes

•

Bright, cheery, and as bountiful as a summer garden, this pretty dish offers a tempting taste of the Mediterranean.

It's seasoned with thyme and plenty of lemon juice; chopped black olives and feta cheese make tangy garnishes.

- 2   teaspoons olive oil
- 1   large onion, chopped
- 1   pound (455 g) mushrooms, thinly sliced
- 1½   pounds (680 g) yellow crookneck squash or yellow zucchini, cut crosswise into ¼-inch (6-mm) slices
- 1½   tablespoons fresh thyme leaves or 1½ teaspoons dried thyme
- 3   tablespoons (45 ml) lemon juice
- 6   medium-size firm-ripe pear-shaped (Roma-type) tomatoes (about 1 lb./455 g *total*), cut crosswise into ¼-inch (6-mm) slices
- ½   cup (50 g) thinly sliced green onions
- 1   ounce (30 g) feta cheese, crumbled
- 2   oil-cured black olives, pitted and chopped

Heat 1 teaspoon of the oil in a wide nonstick frying pan or wok over medium-high heat. When oil is hot, add half *each* of the chopped onion, mushrooms, squash, and thyme. Stir-fry until squash is hot and bright in color (about 3 minutes).

Add ¼ cup (60 ml) water and 1½ tablespoons (23 ml) of the lemon juice to pan; cover and cook until vegetables are just tender to bite (about 3 minutes). Uncover and continue to cook, stirring, until liquid has evaporated (about 3 more minutes). Remove vegetables from pan and set aside.

Repeat to cook remaining chopped onion, mushrooms, squash, and thyme, using remaining 1 teaspoon oil; add ¼ cup (60 ml) water and remaining 1½ tablespoons (23 ml) lemon juice after the first 3 minutes of cooking.

Return all cooked vegetables to pan; gently stir in tomatoes. Transfer vegetables to a serving dish; sprinkle with green onions, cheese, and olives. Makes 8 servings.

Per serving: 78 calories (28% calories from fat), 3 g protein, 12 g carbohydrates, 3 g total fat (1 g saturated fat), 3 mg cholesterol, 72 mg sodium

••

Sprinkled with feta cheese and olives, Mediterranean Squash (recipe at left) is an attractive contribution to a backyard barbecue. Try it with grilled chicken or fish.

Appetizers

....

Assemble-your-own appetizers like the two on this page are perfect for casual gatherings. Start by making a spicy chicken or ground-beef stir-fry; then offer pita quarters or crisp lettuce cups to hold the warm, savory filling.

Thai Chicken in Pitas

Preparation time: About 20 minutes, plus 1 hour for Cilantro Mustard to stand

Cooking time: 3 to 4 minutes

•

Cilantro Mustard (recipe follows)

4 cloves garlic, minced

3 tablespoons minced cilantro

½ teaspoon coarsely ground pepper

1 pound (455 g) boneless, skinless chicken breast, cut into ½-inch (1-cm) pieces

1 teaspoon olive oil or salad oil

4 pita breads (*each* about 6 inches/15 cm in diameter), cut into quarters

Prepare Cilantro Mustard; set aside.

In a large bowl, mix garlic, cilantro, pepper, and chicken. Heat oil in a wide nonstick frying pan or wok over medium-high heat. When oil is hot, add chicken mixture. Stir-fry until meat is no longer pink in center; cut to test (3 to 4 minutes). Add water, 1 tablespoon (15 ml) at a time, if pan appears dry.

With a slotted spoon, transfer chicken to a serving bowl. To eat, spoon chicken into pita breads; driz-

zle chicken with Cilantro Mustard. Makes 6 to 8 servings.

Cilantro Mustard. In a 1- to 1½-quart (950-ml to 1.4-liter) pan, stir together 3 tablespoons **dry mustard,** 3 tablespoons (45 ml) **distilled white vinegar** or white wine vinegar, and 2 tablespoons (30 ml) **water;** cover and let stand for 1 hour.

Mix 3 tablespoons **sugar** and 1 tablespoon **all-purpose flour;** add to mustard mixture along with 3 tablespoons (43 g) **butter** or margarine, cut into chunks. Bring just to a boil over medium-high heat, stirring. Remove from heat and let cool. If made ahead, cover airtight and refrigerate for up to 4 days. Just before serving, stir in 1 to 2 tablespoons chopped **cilantro.**

Per serving: 255 calories (27% calories from fat), 19 g protein, 27 g carbohydrates, 8 g total fat (3 g saturated fat), 51 mg cholesterol, 277 mg sodium

Curry Beef in Lettuce

Preparation time: About 15 minutes

Cooking time: About 15 minutes

•

1 teaspoon cornstarch

6 tablespoons (90 ml) cider vinegar

3 large firm-ripe pears (about 1½ lbs./680 g *total*)

12 ounces (340 g) lean ground beef

4 ounces (115 g) mushrooms, chopped

½ cup (75 g) golden raisins

¼ cup (55 g) firmly packed brown sugar

2 tablespoons *each* curry powder and tomato paste

½ teaspoon ground cinnamon

¼ cup (25 g) sliced green onions

2 tablespoons chopped parsley

½ cup (120 ml) plain nonfat yogurt

1 head butter lettuce (about 6 oz./170 g), separated into leaves, rinsed, and crisped

Salt

In a large bowl, blend cornstarch with 2 tablespoons (30 ml) of the vinegar. Peel, core, and finely chop pears; gently stir into vinegar mixture and set aside.

Crumble beef into a wide nonstick frying pan or wok; add mushrooms and raisins. Stir-fry over medium-high heat until meat is browned (about 8 minutes). Add water, 1 tablespoon (15 ml) at a time, if pan appears dry. Spoon off and discard fat from pan.

Stir in sugar, ¼ cup (60 ml) water, remaining ¼ cup (60 ml) vinegar, curry powder, tomato paste, and cinnamon. Bring to a boil; then stir until almost all liquid has evaporated (about 3 minutes). Add pear mixture; stir until mixture boils and thickens slightly. Transfer to a serving bowl; stir in onions and parsley.

To eat, spoon meat mixture and yogurt into lettuce leaves; season to taste with salt. Makes 4 to 6 servings.

Per serving: 319 calories (21% calories from fat), 18 g protein, 50 g carbohydrates, 8 g total fat (3 g saturated fat), 43 mg cholesterol, 129 mg sodium

Oriental Winter Salad

Preparation time: About 15 minutes
Cooking time: About 25 minutes

•

This warm, crunchy offering is nice for winter days.

- 6 **cups (about 6 oz./170 g) lightly packed rinsed, crisped spinach leaves**
- ¼ **cup (60 ml) unseasoned rice vinegar or white wine vinegar**
- 2 **tablespoons (30 ml) reduced-sodium soy sauce**
- 2 **teaspoons honey**
- 1 **teaspoon Oriental sesame oil**
- 2 **teaspoons sesame seeds**
- 2 **teaspoons salad oil**
- 5 **cups (355 g) broccoli flowerets**
- 1 **pound (455 g) carrots, cut into ¼-inch (6-mm) slanting slices**
- 1½ **cups (180 g) thinly sliced celery**
- 1 **medium-size onion, thinly sliced**

Arrange spinach leaves on a large platter; cover and set aside. In a small bowl, stir together vinegar, soy sauce, honey, and sesame oil; set aside.

In a wide nonstick frying pan or wok, stir sesame seeds over medium heat until golden (about 3 minutes). Pour out of pan and set aside. Heat 1 teaspoon of the salad oil in pan over medium-high heat. When oil is hot, add half *each* of the broccoli, carrots, celery, and onion. Stir-fry until vegetables are hot and bright in color (about 3 minutes). Add ⅓ cup (80 ml) water to pan, cover, and cook until vegetables are just tender to bite (about 3 minutes). Uncover and continue to cook, stirring, until liquid has evaporated (1 to 2 more minutes). Remove vegetables from pan and set aside. Repeat to cook remaining broccoli, carrots, celery, and onion, using remaining 1 teaspoon salad oil and adding ⅓ cup (80 ml) water after the first 3 minutes of cooking.

Return all cooked vegetables to pan and stir in vinegar mixture. Spoon vegetables onto spinach-lined platter and sprinkle with sesame seeds. Makes 6 servings.

Per serving: 118 calories (22% calories from fat), 6 g protein, 20 g carbohydrates, 3 g total fat (0.4 g saturated fat), 0 mg cholesterol, 297 mg sodium

Sautéed Mushrooms with Apple Eau de Vie

Preparation time: About 15 minutes
Cooking time: About 10 minutes

•

Colorless, potent, and redolent of pure ripe fruit, eaux de vie are essentially brandies—but unlike brandies, they aren't aged. A tablespoon of apple eau de vie (or more, if you like) adds a subtle accent to this woodsy-tasting sauté of chanterelles and button mushrooms. Don't forget the salt—just a pinch really helps bring out the flavors.

- 8 **ounces (230 g) *each* fresh chanterelle mushrooms and large regular mushrooms**
- 1 **teaspoon butter or margarine**
- 4 **cloves garlic, minced or pressed**
- 1½ **teaspoons chopped fresh thyme or ½ teaspoon dried thyme**
  About ⅛ teaspoon salt, or to taste
- 1 **tablespoon (15 ml) apple eau de vie or apple brandy, or to taste**
- 1 **tablespoon (15 ml) cream sherry, or to taste**
  Thyme sprigs
  Pepper

Rinse mushrooms and scrub gently, if needed; pat dry. Cut into ¼- to ½-inch-thick (6-mm- to 1-cm-thick) slices; set aside.

Melt butter in a wide nonstick frying pan or wok over medium-high heat. Add garlic and chopped thyme; stir-fry just until fragrant (about 30 seconds; do not scorch). Add mushrooms and ¼ cup (60 ml) water; stir-fry until mushrooms are soft and almost all liquid has evaporated (about 8 minutes). Then add salt and ¼ cup (60 ml) more water; stir-fry until liquid has evaporated (about 2 minutes). Add eau de vie and sherry; stir-fry until liquid has evaporated. Spoon into a serving bowl and garnish with thyme sprigs. Season to taste with pepper. Makes 4 servings.

Per serving: 58 calories (23% calories from fat), 3 g protein, 8 g carbohydrates, 1 g total fat (0.7 g saturated fat), 3 mg cholesterol, 85 mg sodium

Garlic & Rosemary Green Beans

Pictured on facing page
Preparation time: About 10 minutes
Cooking time: About 7 minutes

•

Great-tasting, pretty to look at, very easy to make . . . this dish is a winner. Use the slimmest, most tender green beans you can find.

¼ to ½ ounce (8 to 15 g) prosciutto or bacon, chopped

1 or 2 cloves garlic, minced or pressed

1½ teaspoons chopped fresh rosemary or ½ teaspoon dried rosemary

1 pound (455 g) slender green beans, ends removed

About ⅛ teaspoon salt, or to taste

Rosemary sprigs

Pepper

In a wide nonstick frying pan or wok, stir-fry prosciutto over medium-high heat just until crisp (about 1 minute). Remove from pan with a slotted spoon and set aside.

Add garlic, chopped rosemary, and 2 tablespoons (30 ml) water to pan. Stir-fry just until garlic is fragrant (about 30 seconds; do not scorch). Add beans, ⅓ cup (80 ml) water, and salt. Cover and cook just until beans are tender to bite (about 3 minutes). Uncover and stir-fry until liquid has evaporated. Arrange beans on a rimmed platter, sprinkle with prosciutto, and garnish with rosemary sprigs. Season to taste with pepper. Makes 4 servings.

Per serving: 39 calories (10% calories from fat), 3 g protein, 7 g carbohydrates, 0.5 g total fat (0.1 g saturated fat), 2 mg cholesterol, 125 mg sodium

• •

Aromatic herbs and crisp prosciutto flavor these Garlic & Rosemary Green Beans (recipe above). You might serve them with Sausage, Basil & Port Fettuccine (recipe on page 76) or Chile Beef Stir-fry (recipe on page 73).

Asian-style Green Beans

Preparation time: About 20 minutes
Cooking time: About 15 minutes

•

Cooking green beans with mushrooms is nothing new, but this dish may surprise you with its seasonings—soy sauce, garlic, and a touch of honey—and its topping of crunchy peanuts.

1 medium-size onion, chopped

8 ounces (230 g) mushrooms, sliced

1 medium-size red bell pepper (about 6 oz./170 g), seeded and cut into ¼-inch-wide (6-mm-wide) strips

1 clove garlic, minced or pressed

3 tablespoons (45 ml) reduced-sodium soy sauce

1 tablespoon (15 ml) honey

1 pound (455 g) slender green beans, ends removed

¼ cup (36 g) salted roasted peanuts, chopped

In a wide nonstick frying pan or wok, combine onion, mushrooms, bell pepper, garlic, and ¼ cup (60 ml) water. Stir-fry over medium-high heat until mushrooms are soft and almost all liquid has evaporated (about 10 minutes). Add water, 1 tablespoon (15 ml) at a time, if pan appears dry. Stir soy sauce and honey into mushroom mixture; then transfer to a bowl and keep warm. Wipe pan clean (be careful; pan is hot).

To pan, add beans and ⅓ cup (80 ml) water. Cover and cook over medium-high heat just until beans are tender to bite (about 3 minutes). Uncover and stir-fry until liquid has evaporated.

Arrange beans on a rimmed platter; spoon mushroom mixture over beans and sprinkle with peanuts. Makes 4 to 6 servings.

Per serving: 118 calories (27% calories from fat), 6 g protein, 18 g carbohydrates, 4 g total fat (0.5 g saturated fat), 0 mg cholesterol, 400 mg sodium

Italian-style Swiss Chard

Preparation time: About 15 minutes
Cooking time: About 8 minutes

•

Balsamic vinegar livens up this simple stir-fry. You can make the dish with red or green Swiss chard; or try a combination of both types.

2½   **pounds (1.15 kg) Swiss chard**
2   **teaspoons olive oil**
2   **cloves garlic, minced or pressed**
2   **tablespoons (30 ml) balsamic vinegar**
1   **tablespoon drained capers**

Trim and discard discolored stem ends from chard; then rinse and drain chard. Thinly slice chard stems crosswise up to base of leaves; set aside. Use a few whole leaves to line a large platter; cover and set aside. Coarsely chop remaining leaves.

Heat oil in a wide nonstick frying pan or wok over medium-high heat. When oil is hot, add garlic and chard stems. Stir-fry until stems are soft (about 2 minutes). Add half the chopped chard leaves to pan, cover, and cook for 2 minutes. Add remaining leaves, cover, and cook until all leaves are wilted (about 2 more minutes). Uncover pan and stir in vinegar and capers; then spoon mixture over whole chard leaves on platter. Makes 6 servings.

Per serving: 51 calories (28% calories from fat), 3 g protein, 8 g carbohydrates, 2 g total fat (0.2 g saturated fat), 0 mg cholesterol, 440 mg sodium

Mediterranean Spinach

Preparation time: About 15 minutes
Cooking time: About 10 minutes

•

Fresh dill brings a pleasant, mildly tart flavor to this attractive side dish. Garnishes of feta cheese and capers add that all-important zing—without a lot of fat.

½   **cup (50 g) thinly sliced green onions**
1   **clove garlic, minced or pressed**
1½   **teaspoons chopped fresh dill or ½ teaspoon dried dill weed**
2   **medium-size firm-ripe pear-shaped (Roma-type) tomatoes (about 6 oz./170 g *total*), chopped**
1¼   **pounds (565 g) spinach, stems removed, leaves rinsed and drained**
3   **to 4 tablespoons (25 to 35 g) crumbled feta cheese**
1   **tablespoon drained capers, or to taste**
    Pepper

In a wide nonstick frying pan or wok, combine onions, garlic, dill, and ¼ cup (60 ml) water. Stir-fry over medium-high heat until onions are soft and almost all liquid has evaporated (about 3 minutes). Transfer mixture to a bowl and stir in tomatoes. Keep warm.

Add half the spinach and 1 tablespoon (15 ml) water to pan; stir-fry over medium heat until spinach is just beginning to wilt. Then add remaining spinach; stir-fry just until all spinach is wilted (about 2 more minutes).

With a slotted spoon, transfer spinach to a rimmed platter and spread out slightly; discard liquid from pan. Top spinach with tomato mixture, then sprinkle with cheese and capers. Season to taste with pepper. Makes 4 to 6 servings.

Per serving: 44 calories (29% calories from fat), 7 g protein, 5 g carbohydrates, 2 g total fat (0.9 g saturated fat), 5 mg cholesterol, 179 mg sodium

Low-fat Lo Mein

Preparation time: About 15 minutes
Cooking time: About 15 minutes

•

If you're planning a banquet of Asian-inspired offerings, don't leave out this colorful medley of noodles, vegetables, and browned ground turkey. The combination of textures and tastes—soft with crisp, sweet with salty—makes the dish memorable.

- 12 **ounces (340 g) fresh Chinese noodles or linguine**
- 1 **teaspoon Oriental sesame oil**
- 1 **tablespoon (15 ml) salad oil**
- 1 **small onion, thinly sliced lengthwise**
- 2 **tablespoons (30 ml) oyster sauce**
- 8 **ounces (230 g) ground turkey**
- 1 **pound (455 g) napa cabbage, thinly sliced crosswise**
- 4 **ounces (115 g) oyster mushrooms, thinly sliced**
- 2 **medium-size carrots (about 8 oz./230 g *total*), cut into matchstick strips**
- ½ **cup (120 ml) fat-free reduced-sodium chicken broth**
- 2 **tablespoons (30 ml) reduced-sodium soy sauce**

In a 5- to 6-quart (5- to 6-liter) pan, cook noodles in about 3 quarts (2.8 liters) boiling water until just tender to bite (3 to 5 minutes); or cook according to package directions. Drain well, toss with sesame oil, and keep warm.

Heat salad oil in a wide nonstick frying pan or wok over medium-high heat. When oil is hot, add onion and oyster sauce; then crumble in turkey. Stir-fry until onion is soft and turkey is no longer pink (about 3 minutes). Add cabbage, mushrooms, carrots, and broth; cover and cook until carrots are just tender to bite (about 3 minutes). Uncover and continue to cook until liquid has evaporated (1 to 2 more minutes). Stir in soy sauce; add noodles and stir-fry until heated through. Makes 6 servings.

Per serving: 295 calories (23% calories from fat), 16 g protein, 41 g carbohydrates, 7 g total fat (1 g saturated fat), 69 mg cholesterol, 563 mg sodium

Pork Fried Rice

Preparation time: About 10 minutes
Cooking time: About 10 minutes

•

Fresh ginger, meaty shiitake mushrooms, and bright vegetables give this side dish its savory appeal. For best results, use cooked rice that has been cooled thoroughly.

- 1 **tablespoon salad oil**
- 1 **clove garlic, minced or pressed**
- ½ **teaspoon minced fresh ginger**
- ½ **cup (50 g) thinly sliced green onions**
- 4 **ounces (115 g) lean ground pork**
- 8 **fresh shiitake mushrooms (about 2 oz./55 g *total*), stems removed and caps thinly sliced**
- ½ **cup (75 g) *each* frozen peas and frozen corn kernels, thawed and drained**
- ½ **cup (120 ml) fat-free reduced-sodium chicken broth**
- 2 **tablespoons (30 ml) reduced-sodium soy sauce**
- 3 **cups (390 g) cooked, cooled long-grain white rice**

Heat oil in a wide nonstick frying pan or wok over medium-high heat. When oil is hot, add garlic, ginger, and onions; then crumble in pork. Stir-fry until pork is browned (about 5 minutes).

Add mushrooms, peas, corn, and ¼ cup (60 ml) of the broth to pan; stir-fry until liquid has evaporated (about 2 minutes). Add remaining ¼ cup (60 ml) broth; then stir in soy sauce and rice. Stir-fry until rice is heated through. Makes 6 servings.

Per serving: 235 calories (27% calories from fat), 8 g protein, 35 g carbohydrates, 7 g total fat (2 g saturated fat), 14 mg cholesterol, 282 mg sodium

Broccoli & Bell Pepper with Couscous

Preparation time: About 15 minutes
Cooking time: About 15 minutes

•

Universally lauded by nutritionists, broccoli is a popular choice at the dinner table these days. In this quick dish, the bright, tender flowerets are teamed with bell pepper and served over couscous.

1½ cups (360 ml) fat-free reduced-sodium chicken broth (or use canned vegetable broth)

¼ to ½ teaspoon dried oregano

1 cup (185 g) couscous

1 tablespoon pine nuts or slivered almonds

4 cups (285 g) broccoli flowerets

1 teaspoon olive oil or salad oil

1 small red bell pepper (about 4 oz./115 g), seeded and cut into thin slivers

2 tablespoons (30 ml) balsamic vinegar

In a 3- to 4-quart (2.8- to 3.8-liter) pan, combine broth and oregano. Bring to a boil over high heat; stir in couscous. Cover, remove from heat, and let stand until liquid has been absorbed (about 5 minutes). Transfer couscous to a rimmed platter and keep warm; fluff occasionally with a fork.

While couscous is standing, stir pine nuts in a wide nonstick frying pan or wok over medium-low heat until golden (2 to 4 minutes). Pour out of pan and set aside. To pan, add broccoli and ¼ cup (60 ml) water. Cover and cook over medium-high heat until broccoli is tender-crisp to bite (about 5 minutes). Uncover and stir-fry until liquid has evaporated. Spoon broccoli over couscous and keep warm.

Heat oil in pan. When oil is hot, add bell pepper and stir-fry until just tender-crisp to bite (2 to 3 minutes). Add vinegar to pan and remove from heat; stir to scrape any browned bits free from pan bottom. Immediately pour pepper mixture over broccoli and couscous; sprinkle with pine nuts and serve. Makes 4 servings.

Per serving: 248 calories (10% calories from fat), 12 g protein, 45 g carbohydrates, 3 g total fat (0.4 g saturated fat), 0 mg cholesterol, 278 mg sodium

Curry-glazed Carrots

Pictured on facing page
Preparation time: About 20 minutes
Cooking time: About 10 minutes

•

Looking for a side dish to serve with poached fish or chicken? These thin-sliced carrots are a marvelous choice; their natural sweetness is intensified both by quick stir-frying and by a fresh-tasting glaze of orange juice, maple syrup, and curry.

1 tablespoon grated orange peel

¾ cup (180 ml) orange juice

2 tablespoons (30 ml) maple syrup

2 teaspoons cornstarch blended with 2 tablespoons (30 ml) cold water

1 teaspoon curry powder

1¼ pounds (565 g) carrots, cut diagonally into ¼-inch (6-mm) slices

2 tablespoons minced parsley

Salt and pepper

In a bowl, stir together orange peel, orange juice, syrup, and cornstarch mixture; set aside.

In a wide nonstick frying pan or wok, stir curry powder over medium-high heat just until fragrant (about 30 seconds; do not scorch). Add carrots and ⅓ cup (80 ml) water. Cover and cook just until carrots are tender when pierced (about 4 minutes). Uncover and stir-fry until liquid has evaporated. Stir orange juice mixture well; then pour into pan and cook, stirring, until sauce boils and thickens slightly. Pour carrots and sauce into a serving bowl and sprinkle with parsley. Season to taste with salt and pepper. Makes 4 servings.

Per serving: 117 calories (3% calories from fat), 2 g protein, 28 g carbohydrates, 0.4 g total fat (0 g saturated fat), 0 mg cholesterol, 52 mg sodium

••

Glistening with a sweet maple-orange sauce, mildly spicy Curry-glazed Carrots (recipe above) make a vivid side dish. A sprinkling of minced parsley is a simple, fresh finishing touch.

Stir-fried Salads

*I*deal for chilly-weather dinners, the salads on these two pages are just as good in summer: because the cooking times are so brief, you can serve a warm entrée without overheating the kitchen (or yourself). All of our selections feature crisp greens topped with a savory stir-fry; choose Asian-seasoned chicken, spicy sausage with ripe pears, shrimp and crab in a lemony dressing, or thin-sliced pork loin with apples. For best results, serve stir-fried salads at once, just as soon as the greens are slightly wilted from the heat of the topping.

Warm Chinese Chicken Salad

Preparation time: About 15 minutes
Cooking time: About 5 minutes

•

⅓ cup (80 ml) seasoned rice vinegar (or ⅓ cup/80 ml distilled white vinegar plus 2 teaspoons sugar)

1 tablespoon (15 ml) reduced-sodium soy sauce

1½ teaspoons *each* sugar and Oriental sesame oil

7 cups (about 7 oz./200g) finely shredded iceberg lettuce

3 cups (about 3 oz./ 85 g) bite-size pieces of radicchio

⅓ cup (15 g) lightly packed cilantro leaves

¼ cup (25 g) sliced green onions

1 pound (455 g) boneless, skinless chicken breast, cut into thin strips

2 cloves garlic, minced or pressed
  Cilantro sprigs

In a small bowl, stir together vinegar, 1 tablespoon (15 ml) water, soy sauce, sugar, and oil; set aside.

In a large serving bowl, combine lettuce, radicchio, cilantro leaves, and onions; cover and set aside.

In a wide nonstick frying pan or wok, combine chicken, 1 tablespoon (15 ml) water, and garlic. Stir-fry

over medium-high heat until chicken is no longer pink in center; cut to test (3 to 4 minutes). Add water, 1 tablespoon (15 ml) at a time, if pan appears dry. Add vinegar mixture to pan and bring to a boil. Quickly pour chicken and sauce over greens, then mix gently but thoroughly. Garnish with cilantro sprigs and serve immediately. Makes 4 servings.

Per serving: 185 calories (17% calories from fat), 28 g protein, 10 g carbohydrates, 3 g total fat (0.6 g saturated fat), 66 mg cholesterol, 626 mg sodium

Warm Spinach, Pear & Sausage Salad

Preparation time: About 15 minutes
Cooking time: About 15 minutes

•

3 green onions

8 ounces (230 g) spinach, stems removed, leaves rinsed and crisped

1 large yellow or red bell pepper (about 8 oz./230 g), seeded and cut lengthwise into thin strips

5 medium-size firm-ripe pears (1¾ to 2 lbs./795 to 905 g *total*)

1 teaspoon olive oil or salad oil

8 to 10 ounces (230 to 285 g) mild or hot turkey Italian sausages, casings removed

⅓ cup (80 ml) balsamic vinegar

¾ teaspoon fennel seeds

Trim and discard ends of onions. Cut onions into 2-inch (5-cm) lengths; then cut each piece lengthwise into slivers. Tear spinach into bite-size pieces. Place onions, spinach, and bell pepper in a large serving bowl, cover, and set aside.

Peel and core pears; slice thinly. Heat oil in a wide nonstick frying pan or wok over medium-high heat. When oil is hot, add pears and stir-fry until almost tender to bite (about 5 minutes). Lift pears from pan with a slotted spoon; transfer to a bowl and keep warm.

Crumble sausage into pan and stir-fry over medium-high heat until browned (5 to 7 minutes); add water, 1 tablespoon (15 ml) at a time, if pan appears dry. Add pears, vinegar, and fennel seeds to pan. Stir gently to mix, scraping browned bits free from pan bottom. Immediately pour hot pear mixture over spinach mixture; toss gently but thoroughly until spinach is slightly wilted. Serve immediately. Makes 4 servings.

Per serving: 261 calories (29% calories from fat), 13 g protein, 37 g carbohydrates, 9 g total fat (2 g saturated fat), 34 mg cholesterol, 454 mg sodium

Warm Cioppino Salad

Preparation time: About 20 minutes
Cooking time: About 10 minutes

•

Lemon Dressing (recipe follows)

3 **quarts (about 12 oz./340 g) lightly packed rinsed, crisped spinach leaves, torn into bite-size pieces**

1 **tablespoon (15 ml) olive oil**

8 **ounces (230 g) extra-large raw shrimp (26 to 30 per lb.), shelled and deveined**

2 **cups (170 g) sliced mushrooms (¼ inch/6 mm thick)**

2 **cups (340 g) sliced zucchini (¼ inch/6 mm thick)**

1 **can (about 14½ oz./415 g) tomatoes, drained and chopped; or 1½ cups (235 g) chopped fresh tomatoes**

12 **pitted ripe olives**

8 **ounces (230 g) cooked crabmeat**

Prepare Lemon Dressing and set aside. Place spinach in a wide serving bowl, cover, and set aside.

Heat oil in a wide nonstick frying pan or wok over medium-high heat.

When oil is hot, add shrimp and stir-fry until just opaque in center; cut to test (3 to 4 minutes). Remove from pan with tongs or a slotted spoon and set aside.

Add mushrooms and zucchini to pan; stir-fry until zucchini is just tender to bite (about 3 minutes). Return shrimp to pan; add tomatoes, olives, and Lemon Dressing. Stir until mixture is heated through. Quickly pour shrimp mixture over spinach, top with crab, and mix gently but thoroughly. Serve immediately. Makes 6 servings.

Lemon Dressing. In a small bowl, stir together ¼ cup (60 ml) **lemon juice,** 1 teaspoon *each* **dried basil** and **dried oregano,** and 2 cloves **garlic,** minced or pressed.

Per serving: 149 calories (28% calories from fat), 18 g protein, 10 g carbohydrates, 5 g total fat (0.7 g saturated fat), 85 mg cholesterol, 380 mg sodium

Stir-fried Pork & Escarole Salad

Preparation time: About 25 minutes
Cooking time: About 5 minutes

•

3 **quarts (about 12 oz./340 g) lightly packed rinsed, crisped escarole or spinach leaves**

⅔ **cup (160 ml) cider vinegar**

3 **tablespoons (45 ml) honey**

2 **large Red Delicious apples (about 1 lb./455 g *total*), cored and thinly sliced**

4 **teaspoons cornstarch**

1 **cup (240 ml) fat-free reduced-sodium chicken broth**

2 **teaspoons Dijon mustard**

½ **teaspoon dried thyme**

2 **teaspoons olive oil**

2 **large shallots, chopped**

1 **pound (455 g) lean boneless pork loin, loin end, or leg, trimmed of fat and cut into paper-thin ½- by 3-inch (1- by 8-cm) slices**

1 **cup (145 g) raisins**

Place escarole on a wide platter. In a medium-size bowl, stir together vinegar, honey, and apples. Then remove apples with a slotted spoon and scatter over escarole. Add cornstarch, broth, mustard, and thyme to vinegar mixture in bowl; stir well and set aside.

Heat oil in a wide nonstick frying pan or wok over medium-high heat. When oil is hot, add shallots and pork and stir-fry until meat is lightly browned (about 3 minutes). Push meat to one side of pan. Stir vinegar mixture well, pour into pan, and stir just until boiling (about 1 minute). Stir meat into sauce; then quickly spoon meat mixture over escarole and sprinkle with raisins. Serve immediately. Makes 4 servings.

Per serving: 443 calories (18% calories from fat), 28 g protein, 67 g carbohydrates, 10 g total fat (3 g saturated fat), 67 mg cholesterol, 320 mg sodium

Stir-fried Herbed Cauliflower

Preparation time: About 15 minutes
Cooking time: About 10 minutes

•

If you like cauliflower, garlic, and basil, you'll enjoy this robust stir-fry; it's a good addition to a late-summer menu. Sliced zucchini and diced tomatoes offer a nice color contrast to the creamy-pale cauliflower.

- 2 teaspoons olive oil
- 1 large cauliflower (about 2 lbs./905 g), cut into bite-size flowerets
- 2 cloves garlic, minced or pressed
- 1 large onion, chopped
- 8 ounces (230 g) small zucchini, cut crosswise into ¼-inch (6-mm) slices
- ⅓ cup (80 ml) dry white wine
- 3 medium-size firm-ripe pear-shaped (Roma-type) tomatoes (about 8 oz./230 g *total*), chopped
- 1 tablespoon chopped fresh basil

Heat oil in a wide nonstick frying pan or wok over medium-high heat. When oil is hot, add cauliflower, garlic, onion, and zucchini; stir-fry until zucchini is hot and bright in color (2 to 3 minutes).

Add wine, tomatoes, and basil to pan. Cover and cook until cauliflower is just tender to bite (about 4 minutes). Uncover and continue to cook until liquid has evaporated (2 to 3 more minutes). Makes 4 servings.

Per serving: 93 calories (27% calories from fat), 4 g protein, 13 g carbohydrates, 3 g total fat (0.4 g saturated fat), 0 mg cholesterol, 23 mg sodium

....

Put thick salmon steaks on the grill—then assemble colorful Tricolor Pepper Sauté (recipe at right). This fresh and easy dish combines fluffy rice with crisp bean sprouts and thin strips of red, yellow, and green bell pepper.

Tricolor Pepper Sauté

Pictured on facing page
Preparation time: About 15 minutes
Cooking time: About 25 minutes

•

This colorful side dish is guaranteed to brighten up any menu. Simply spoon stir-fried, ginger-seasoned yellow, red, and green bell peppers over hot rice; you can make the topping while the rice is cooking.

- 1 cup (185 g) long-grain white rice
- 1 to 2 teaspoons sesame seeds
- 3 medium-size bell peppers (1 to 1¼ lbs./455 to 565 g *total*); use 1 *each* red, yellow, and green bell pepper
- 1 teaspoon salad oil
- 1 small onion, cut into thin slivers
- 1 tablespoon minced fresh ginger
- 1 clove garlic, minced or pressed
- 1 cup (85 g) bean sprouts
- 2 teaspoons Oriental sesame oil
  Reduced-sodium soy sauce or salt

In a 3- to 4-quart (2.8- to 3.8-liter) pan, bring 2 cups (470 ml) water to a boil over high heat; stir in rice. Reduce heat, cover, and simmer until liquid has been absorbed and rice is tender to bite (about 20 minutes).

Meanwhile, in a wide nonstick frying pan or wok, stir sesame seeds over medium heat until golden (about 3 minutes). Pour out of pan and set aside.

Seed bell peppers and cut into thin slivers, 2 to 3 inches (5 to 8 cm) long. Heat salad oil in pan over medium-high heat. When oil is hot, add onion, ginger, and garlic; stir-fry for 1 minute. Add peppers; stir-fry until tender-crisp to bite (about 3 minutes). Add bean sprouts and stir-fry until barely wilted (about 1 minute). Remove from heat and stir in sesame oil.

Spoon rice onto a rimmed platter; pour vegetable mixture over rice and sprinkle with sesame seeds. Offer soy sauce to add to taste. Makes 4 servings.

Per serving: 253 calories (16% calories from fat), 5 g protein, 48 g carbohydrates, 4 g total fat (0.7 g saturated fat), 0 mg cholesterol, 7 mg sodium

Linguine with Yellow Tomatoes

Pictured on page 3
Preparation time: About 15 minutes
Cooking time: About 15 minutes

•

This dish says "summer." Plain and perfect for warm-weather meals, it's a simple combination of tender pasta ribbons, juicy-ripe cherry tomatoes, and fragrant fresh basil leaves.

- 1 **pound (455 g) dried linguine**
  About 2 tablespoons (30 ml) Hot Chili Oil (page 69) or purchased hot chili oil
- 1 **clove garlic, minced or pressed**
- 1 **large onion, chopped**
- 6 **cups (905 g) yellow or red cherry or other tiny tomatoes (or use some of each color), cut into halves**
- 2 **cups (80 g) firmly packed fresh basil leaves**
  Basil sprigs (optional)
  Grated Parmesan cheese
  Salt

In a 6- to 8-quart (6- to 8-liter) pan, cook linguine in about 4 quarts (3.8 liters) boiling water until just tender to bite (8 to 10 minutes); or cook according to package directions. Drain well, transfer to a warm wide bowl, and keep warm.

While pasta is cooking, heat 2 tablespoons of the chili oil in a wide nonstick frying pan or wok over medium-high heat. When oil is hot, add garlic and onion; stir-fry until onion is soft (about 5 minutes). Add tomatoes and basil leaves; stir gently until tomatoes are heated through (about 2 minutes).

Pour hot tomato mixture over pasta. Garnish with basil sprigs, if desired. Offer cheese to add to taste; season to taste with more chili oil and salt. Makes 6 to 8 servings.

Per serving: 322 calories (15% calories from fat), 10 g protein, 59 g carbohydrates, 5 g total fat (0.7 g saturated fat), 0 mg cholesterol, 18 mg sodium

Vegetable Stir-fry with Soba

Preparation time: About 15 minutes
Cooking time: About 10 minutes

•

Soft buckwheat noodles tossed with tender-crisp vegetables and topped with roasted cashews make a great complement to grilled pork tenderloin.

- **Cooking Sauce (recipe follows)**
- 8 **ounces (230 g) dried soba noodles or capellini**
- 1 **large red or green bell pepper (about 8 oz./230 g), seeded and cut into thin slivers**
- ½ **cup (60 g) thinly sliced celery**
- ½ **cup (50 g) thinly sliced green onions**
- ½ **cup (70 g) salted roasted cashews**

Prepare Cooking Sauce; set aside.

In a 4- to 5-quart (3.8- to 5-liter) pan, cook pasta in about 8 cups (1.9 liters) boiling water until just tender to bite (about 5 minutes for soba, about 3 minutes for capellini); or cook according to package directions. Drain well, transfer to a warm wide bowl, and keep warm.

In a wide nonstick frying pan or wok, combine bell pepper, celery, and ¼ cup (60 ml) water. Stir-fry over high heat until vegetables are tender-crisp to bite and liquid has evaporated (about 5 minutes). Stir Cooking Sauce and pour into pan; bring just to a boil. Pour vegetable mixture over noodles, then add onions and mix gently but thoroughly. Sprinkle with cashews. Makes 4 servings.

Cooking Sauce. In a small bowl, stir together 2 tablespoons (30 ml) *each* **oyster sauce, reduced-sodium soy sauce,** and **lemon juice.** Stir in 1 teaspoon **Oriental sesame oil.**

Per serving: 329 calories (24% calories from fat), 13 g protein, 54 g carbohydrates, 9 g total fat (2 g saturated fat), 0 mg cholesterol, 1,225 mg sodium

Pasta with Artichokes & Anchovies

Preparation time: About 10 minutes
Cooking time: About 15 minutes

•

If you like sharp, savory flavors, this dish is for you. Hot linguine is tossed with a sauce of marinated artichoke hearts, ripe olives, anchovy paste, and a little grated Parmesan cheese.

    8 ounces (230 g) dried linguine
    1 jar (about 6 oz./170 g) marinated artichoke hearts
    2 cloves garlic, minced or pressed
    1 tablespoon anchovy paste
    1 can (about 2¼ oz./65 g) sliced ripe olives, drained
    ½ cup (30 g) chopped parsley
    ¼ cup (20 g) grated Parmesan cheese
       Parsley sprigs
       Pepper

In a 4- to 5-quart (3.8- to 5-liter) pan, cook linguine in about 8 cups (1.9 liters) boiling water until just tender to bite (8 to 10 minutes); or cook according to package directions. Drain well, transfer to a warm wide bowl, and keep warm.

While pasta is cooking, carefully drain marinade from artichokes into a wide nonstick frying pan or wok. Cut artichokes into bite-size pieces and set aside. Heat marinade over medium heat; add garlic and stir-fry until pale gold (about 3 minutes). Add anchovy paste, olives, and artichokes; stir-fry until heated through (about 2 minutes).

Pour artichoke mixture over pasta. Add chopped parsley and cheese; mix gently but thoroughly. Garnish with parsley sprigs; season to taste with pepper. Makes 4 to 6 servings.

Per serving: 245 calories (23% calories from fat), 10 g protein, 38 g carbohydrates, 6 g total fat (1 g saturated fat), 5 mg cholesterol, 499 mg sodium

Indian Potatoes

Preparation time: About 10 minutes
Cooking time: About 15 minutes

•

Potato lovers are sure to delight in this dish. To make it, you cook potato slices and sweet red pepper with Indian-style seasonings of cumin, chili, and coriander, then top the combination with fresh cilantro and a big spoonful of cool, tart sour cream.

    1¼ pounds (565 g) small red thin-skinned potatoes, scrubbed
     2 tablespoons (30 g) butter or margarine
     1 medium-size red bell pepper (about 6 oz./170 g), seeded and cut into thin slivers
     1 medium-size onion, cut into thin slivers
     1 tablespoon ground cumin
     1 teaspoon ground coriander
     ¼ teaspoon Hot Chili Oil (page 69) or purchased hot chili oil, or to taste
     ⅓ cup (15 g) chopped cilantro
     ½ cup (120 ml) nonfat sour cream
        Cilantro sprigs
        Salt

Cut potatoes crosswise into ¼-inch (6-mm) slices. Melt butter in a wide nonstick frying pan or wok over medium-high heat. Add potatoes, bell pepper, onion, cumin, coriander, chili oil, and 3 tablespoons (45 ml) water. Stir-fry gently until potatoes are tinged with brown and tender when pierced (about 15 minutes; do not scorch). Add water, 1 tablespoon (15 ml) at a time, if pan appears dry.

Remove pan from heat. Sprinkle potato mixture with chopped cilantro and mix gently but thoroughly. Spoon into a serving bowl, top with sour cream, and garnish with cilantro sprigs. Season to taste with salt. Makes 4 servings.

Per serving: 220 calories (27% calories from fat), 6 g protein, 34 g carbohydrates, 7 g total fat (4 g saturated fat), 15 mg cholesterol, 94 mg sodium

Asparagus & Pasta Stir-fry

Preparation time: About 10 minutes
Cooking time: About 15 minutes

•

Here's an interesting presentation for fresh asparagus— and a way to make it go a little farther, too.

- 6 ounces (170 g) dried vermicelli
- 1 pound (455 g) asparagus
- 2 teaspoons salad oil
- 1 clove garlic, minced or pressed
- 1 teaspoon minced fresh ginger
- ½ cup (50 g) diagonally sliced green onions
- 2 tablespoons (30 ml) reduced-sodium soy sauce
- ⅛ teaspoon crushed red pepper flakes

In a 4- to 5-quart (3.8- to 5-liter) pan, cook pasta in about 8 cups (1.9 liters) boiling water until just tender to bite (8 to 10 minutes); or cook according to package directions.

Meanwhile, snap off and discard tough ends of asparagus; then cut asparagus into 1½-inch (3.5-cm) slanting slices and set aside. Heat oil in a wide nonstick frying pan or wok over medium-high heat. When oil is hot, add garlic, ginger, asparagus, and onions. Stir-fry until asparagus is tender-crisp to bite (about 3 minutes). Add soy sauce and red pepper flakes; stir-fry for 1 more minute.

Drain pasta well, add to asparagus mixture, and stir-fry until heated through. Makes 4 to 6 servings.

Per serving: 161 calories (14% calories from fat), 6 g protein, 29 g carbohydrates, 2 g total fat (0.3 g saturated fat), 0 mg cholesterol, 245 mg sodium

Sweet Potato Stir-fry

Pictured on facing page
Preparation time: About 15 minutes
Cooking time: About 15 minutes

•

When you're choosing recipes for your holiday table, don't pass up this one. Diced sweet potatoes are stir-fried and sweetened with golden raisins, spices, and coconut;

pomegranate seeds, stirred in at the last minute, are a gleaming, jewel-bright accent.

- 3 large oranges (about 1¾ lbs./795 g *total*)

  About 24 large spinach leaves (about 2 oz./55 g *total*), rinsed and crisped
- ½ cup (120 ml) fat-free reduced-sodium chicken broth (or use canned vegetable broth)
- ½ cup (75 g) golden raisins
- ¼ cup (60 ml) orange juice
- 2 teaspoons honey
- ⅛ teaspoon *each* ground cloves and ground nutmeg
- 2 teaspoons salad oil
- 2 large sweet potatoes or yams (about 1 lb./455 g *total*), peeled and cut into ¼-inch (6-mm) cubes
- ¼ cup (20 g) sweetened shredded coconut
- ⅓ cup (55 g) pomegranate seeds

Cut off and discard peel and all white membrane from oranges; then cut fruit crosswise into thin slices. Cover and set aside. Arrange spinach leaves on a rimmed platter; cover and set aside. In a bowl, stir together broth, raisins, orange juice, honey, cloves, and nutmeg; set aside.

Heat oil in a wide nonstick frying pan or wok over medium-high heat. When oil is hot, add sweet potatoes and 2 tablespoons (30 ml) water; stir-fry until potatoes begin to brown and are just tender-crisp to bite (about 7 minutes). Add water, 1 tablespoon (15 ml) at a time, if pan appears dry. Add broth mixture to pan; cover and cook until potatoes are just tender to bite (about 5 minutes). Uncover and stir-fry until liquid has evaporated. Remove pan from heat and stir in coconut and ¼ cup (40 g) of the pomegranate seeds.

Arrange orange slices over spinach leaves on platter. Spoon potato mixture over oranges; sprinkle with remaining pomegranate seeds. Makes 4 servings.

Per serving: 284 calories (13% calories from fat), 4 g protein, 61 g carbohydrates, 4 g total fat (2 g saturated fat), 0 mg cholesterol, 117 mg sodium

....

Beautifully presented atop orange slices and crisp spinach leaves, Sweet Potato Stir-fry (recipe at left) is a perfect complement for roast turkey or chicken. It's a splendid choice for a holiday menu—and just as delightful for simple family meals.

Cheese & Apple Hash Browns

Preparation time: About 25 minutes
Cooking time: About 20 minutes

•

Hash browns? Yes, but not the standard kind. True, the potatoes are there—but so are Golden Delicious apples, red bell pepper, and aromatic cumin seeds. Sprinkled with Cheddar cheese, the dish is good alongside grilled Canadian bacon or any other favorite partner for hash browns.

- 2 **large Golden Delicious apples (about 1 lb./455 g** *total*)**, peeled, cored, and finely chopped**
- 1 **tablespoon (15 ml) lemon juice**
- 2 **teaspoons butter or margarine**
- 2 **large russet potatoes (about 1 lb./455 g** *total*)**, peeled and cut into ¼-inch (6-mm) cubes**
- 1 **medium-size onion, chopped**
- 1 **medium-size red bell pepper (about 6 oz./170 g), seeded and diced**
- ½ **teaspoon cumin seeds**
- ¼ **cup (15 g) chopped parsley**
- ½ **cup (55 g) shredded reduced-fat sharp Cheddar cheese**

 Salt and pepper

In a medium-size bowl, mix apples and lemon juice. Set aside; stir occasionally.

Melt butter in a wide nonstick frying pan or wok over medium heat. Add potatoes, onion, and bell pepper. Stir-fry until potatoes are tinged with brown and tender when pierced (about 15 minutes). Add water, 1 tablespoon (15 ml) at a time, if pan appears dry.

Stir in apples and cumin seeds; stir-fry until apples are tender to bite (about 5 minutes). Remove pan from heat and stir in parsley; then spoon potato mixture into a serving bowl. Sprinkle with cheese. Season to taste with salt and pepper. Makes 4 to 6 servings.

Per serving: 182 calories (20% calories from fat), 6 g protein, 32 g carbohydrates, 4 g total fat (2 g saturated fat), 12 mg cholesterol, 106 mg sodium

Snow Peas with Bacon & Mint

Preparation time: About 15 minutes
Cooking time: About 10 minutes

•

A lovely and refreshing choice for a family meal, this emerald-green dish features sweet snow peas accented with a light, tart vinegar sauce and a sprinkling of smoky bacon. Be sure to serve at once; upon standing, the pea pods will lose their bright color.

- ¼ **cup (60 ml)** *each* **fat-free reduced-sodium chicken broth and distilled white vinegar**
- 2 **teaspoons sugar**
- 1 **teaspoon cornstarch**
- 2 **thick slices bacon, finely chopped**
- 1 **pound (455 g) fresh Chinese pea pods (also called snow or sugar peas), ends and strings removed; or 3 packages (about 6 oz./170 g** *each*) **frozen Chinese pea pods, thawed and drained**
- 1 **tablespoon chopped fresh mint**

 Mint sprigs

In a small bowl, stir together broth, vinegar, sugar, and cornstarch; set aside.

In a wide nonstick frying pan or wok, stir-fry bacon over medium-high heat until browned and crisp (about 3 minutes). Remove bacon from pan with a slotted spoon and set aside. Pour off and discard drippings from pan. Wipe pan clean (be careful; pan is hot).

Add pea pods and ⅓ cup (80 ml) water to pan. Cover and cook over medium-high heat until pea pods are tender-crisp to bite (about 1 minute for fresh pea pods, about 30 seconds for frozen). Uncover and stir-fry until liquid has evaporated. Transfer to a rimmed platter and keep warm.

Stir broth mixture well; pour into pan. Bring to a boil over high heat; boil, stirring, until slightly thickened. Remove from heat and stir in chopped mint. Pour sauce over pea pods, sprinkle with bacon, and garnish with mint sprigs. Serve immediately. Makes 4 to 6 servings.

Per serving: 73 calories (27% calories from fat), 4 g protein, 10 g carbohydrates, 2 g total fat (0.8 g saturated fat), 4 mg cholesterol, 104 mg sodium

Stir-frying Fresh Vegetables

To stir-fry fresh vegetables:

1. Cut vegetables into uniform slices or small pieces, as directed in the chart below.

2. Heat 2 teaspoons of oil in a wide (12-inch) nonstick frying pan or wok over medium-high heat. When oil is hot, add vegetables all at once and stir-fry, uncovered, for time noted in chart.

3. Add designated amount of liquid (fat-free reduced-sodium chicken broth, vegetable broth, or water). Cover tightly and cook for remaining time noted in chart. As vegetables cook, all or almost all liquid will evaporate. If any liquid remains, uncover pan and stir-fry, uncovered, until all or almost all liquid has evaporated.

Remember that the times noted below should be used as guides. Actual times may vary, depending on the freshness and maturity of the vegetables and on the degree of doneness you prefer. Taste vegetables after the minimum cooking time; if you prefer a softer texture, continue to cook, tasting often, until vegetables are done to your liking.

VEGETABLE (4 cups, cut up)	**WEIGHT** (untrimmed / trimmed)	**SALAD OIL** (teaspoons)	**STIR-FRY** (minutes uncovered)	**LIQUID** (tablespoons)	**COOK** (minutes covered)
Asparagus Cut into 1-inch (2.5-cm) slanting slices	**1½ lbs. (680 g) / 1 lb. (455 g)**	**2**	**1**	**1 (15 ml)**	**2**
Beans, green Cut into 1-inch (2.5-cm) pieces	**1 lb. (455 g) / 15½ oz. (440 g)**	**2**	**1**	**4 (60 ml)**	**4**
Bok choy Cut into ¼-inch (6-mm) slices; shred leaves and add during last 2 minutes of cooking time	**14 oz. (400 g) / 13 oz. (370 g)**	**2**	**1**	**1 (15 ml)**	**3½**
Broccoli Cut into 1-inch (2.5-cm) flowerets	**1¼ lbs. (565 g) / 12 oz. (340 g)**	**2**	**1**	**4 (60 ml)**	**3**
Cabbage *Green or red.* Shredded	**1⅛ lbs. (510 g) / 14 oz. (400 g)**	**2**	**1**	**2 (30 ml)**	**3**
Cabbage *Napa.* Cut white part into 1-inch (2.5-cm) slices; shred leaves and add during last 2 minutes of cooking time	**1 lb. (455 g) / 14 oz. (400 g)**	**2**	**1**	**2 (30 ml)**	**4**
Carrots Cut into ¼-inch (6-mm) slices	**1¾ lbs. (795 g) / 1¼ lbs. (565 g)**	**2**	**1**	**2 (30 ml)**	**4**
Cauliflower Cut into 1-inch (2.5-cm) flowerets	**2 lbs. (905 g) / 1 lb. (455 g)**	**2**	**1**	**4 (60 ml)**	**4**
Celery Cut into ¼-inch (6-mm) slices	**1¼ lbs. (565 g) / 1 lb. (455 g)**	**2**	**1**	**1 (15 ml)**	**3**
Eggplant Cut into ½-inch (1-cm) cubes	**12 oz. (340 g) / 10 oz. (285 g)**	**2**	**1**	**4 (60 ml)**	**3½**
Fennel Cut into ¼-inch (6-mm) slices	**2 lbs. (905 g) / 1 lb. (455 g)**	**2**	**4**	**none**	**none**
Mushrooms Cut into ¼-inch (6-mm) slices	**12 oz. (340 g) / 11½ oz. (325 g)**	**2**	**4**	**none**	**none**
Onions Cut into ¼-inch (6-mm) slices	**1 lb. (455 g) / 14 oz. (400 g)**	**2**	**1**	**2 (30 ml)**	**4**
Pea pods, Chinese	**1 lb. (455 g) / 15 oz. (430 g)**	**2**	**1**	**1 (15 ml)**	**½**
Peppers, bell Cut into 1-inch (2.5-cm) slices	**1 lb. 5oz. (600 g) / 1⅛ lbs. (510 g)**	**2**	**1**	**2 (30 ml)**	**5**
Potatoes *Russet.* Cut into ¼-inch (6-mm) cubes	**1⅜ lbs. (625 g) / 1¼ lbs. (565 g)**	**2**	**1**	**6 (90 ml)**	**6**
Spinach Whole leaves	**12 oz. (340 g) / 4 oz. (115 g)**	**2**	**½**	**none**	**2**
Sprouts, bean	**1 lb. (455 g) / 1 lb. (455 g)**	**2**	**1**	**none**	**½**
Squash, summer Cut into ¼-inch (6-mm) slices	**1 lb. (455 g) / 15½ oz. (440 g)**	**2**	**1**	**2 (30 ml)**	**3**
Swiss chard Cut stems into ¼-inch (6-mm) slices; shred leaves and add during last 2 minutes of cooking time	**8 oz. (230 g) / 8 oz. (230 g)**	**2**	**1**	**1 (15 ml)**	**3½**

Poultry Dishes

Quick-cooking poultry is a natural for stir-frying—and it's wonderfully versatile, too. From fajitas filled with lean turkey breast to an elegant combination of chicken and apples in cream, our recipes are bound to become dinnertime favorites.

....

A light, tart-sweet sauce tops stir-fried chicken breast in our refreshing Lemon Chicken (recipe on page 32). You might complete the meal with short-grain rice, a crisp salad, and cups of hot tea.

Lemon Chicken

Pictured on page 30
Preparation time: About 20 minutes
Cooking time: About 10 minutes

•

Battered, deep-fried chicken topped with a sweet lemon sauce is a popular choice at Chinese restaurants. Our stir-fried interpretation of the dish features strips of boneless chicken breast in a thin, golden crust; the light lemon sauce is deliciously tart-sweet. For a pretty presentation, serve the chicken on a bed of lemon slices.

You'll find that cooking goes most smoothly if you start heating the oil just before you drain the chicken. That way, you can transfer the chicken directly from the batter to the hot wok, with no need to set it aside.

  Cooking Sauce (recipe follows)

3 or 4 large lemons, thinly sliced

2 large egg whites

¾ cup (96 g) cornstarch

¼ cup (30 g) all-purpose flour

1 teaspoon *each* baking powder and finely minced fresh ginger

¼ teaspoon salt (optional)

⅛ teaspoon ground white pepper

1 tablespoon (15 ml) salad oil

1 pound (455 g) boneless, skinless chicken breast, cut into ½- by 3-inch (1- by 8-cm) strips

  Finely shredded lemon peel

  Cilantro sprigs

Prepare Cooking Sauce; set aside. Arrange lemon slices on a rimmed platter, overlapping them if necessary; cover and set aside.

In a large bowl, beat egg whites and ½ cup (120 ml) water to blend. Add cornstarch, flour, baking powder, ginger, salt (if used), and white pepper; stir until smoothly blended.

Heat oil in a wide nonstick frying pan or wok over medium-high heat. Meanwhile, dip chicken pieces in batter. Lift out and drain briefly to let excess batter drip off; discard remaining batter.

When oil is hot, add chicken and stir-fry gently, separating pieces, until meat is lightly browned on outside

and no longer pink in center; cut to test (5 to 7 minutes; if any pieces brown too much, remove them from pan and keep warm). Arrange chicken over lemon slices on platter; keep warm.

Wipe pan clean (be careful; pan is hot). Stir Cooking Sauce well; pour into pan. Stir over medium-high heat until sauce boils and thickens slightly (1 to 2 minutes). Pour sauce over chicken and sprinkle with lemon peel. Garnish with cilantro sprigs. Makes 4 servings.

Cooking Sauce. Finely shred ½ teaspoon peel (colored part only) from 1 or 2 large **lemons;** set peel aside. Squeeze enough juice to measure 3 tablespoons (45 ml). In a small bowl, stir together lemon juice and 1 tablespoon **cornstarch** until blended. Then stir in lemon peel, ⅓ cup (80 ml) **fat-free reduced-sodium chicken broth,** ¼ cup (50 g) **sugar,** 2 tablespoons (30 ml) *each* **light corn syrup** and **distilled white vinegar,** 1 tablespoon (15 ml) **water,** 1 teaspoon **salad oil,** ¼ teaspoon **salt** (optional), and 2 cloves **garlic,** minced or pressed.

Per serving: 368 calories (14% calories from fat), 30 g protein, 56 g carbohydrates, 6 g total fat (1 g saturated fat), 66 mg cholesterol, 245 mg sodium

Chicken with Chanterelle-Tarragon Sauce

Preparation time: About 35 minutes, plus 30 minutes to soak mushrooms
Cooking time: About 25 minutes

•

It's hard to believe that this rich-tasting entrée is low in fat. If you can't find dried chanterelles, just substitute economical button mushrooms.

½ ounce/15 g (about 1 cup) dried chanterelle mushrooms; or 8 ounces (230 g) fresh regular mushrooms, thinly sliced

1½ cups (280 g) long-grain white rice

2 teaspoons butter or olive oil

1 pound (455 g) boneless, skinless chicken breast, cut into ½- by 2-inch (1- by 5-cm) strips

¾ cup (180 ml) fat-free reduced-sodium chicken broth

¼ cup (60 ml) **chardonnay**

2 teaspoons **chopped fresh tarragon or 1 teaspoon dried tarragon**

2 tablespoons (30 ml) **half-and-half**

If using chanterelles, place them in a 1½- to 2-quart (1.4- to 1.9-liter) pan and add 1½ cups (360 ml) water. Bring to a boil over high heat; then reduce heat, cover tightly, and simmer gently until mushrooms are very tender when pierced (about 30 minutes). Remove from heat and let stand for 30 minutes. Then lift chanterelles from water, squeezing liquid from them into pan; reserve water. Set chanterelles aside.

In a 4- to 5-quart (3.8- to 5-liter) pan, bring 3 cups (710 ml) water to a boil over high heat; stir in rice. Reduce heat, cover, and simmer until liquid has been absorbed and rice is tender to bite (about 20 minutes).

Meanwhile, melt butter in a wide nonstick frying pan or wok over medium-high heat. Add chicken and stir-fry until no longer pink in center; cut to test (3 to 4 minutes). Remove chicken from pan with a slotted spoon and keep warm.

Add chanterelles or regular mushrooms to pan; stir-fry until tinged a darker brown (about 5 minutes). Carefully pour reserved cooking water into pan, taking care not to add any grit from mushrooms. Add broth, wine, and tarragon. Bring to a boil; then boil, stirring, until liquid is reduced to ⅓ cup (80 ml). Add half-and-half; cook, stirring, until mixture returns to a boil. Remove from heat and stir in chicken.

Spoon rice onto a rimmed platter; spoon chicken mixture over rice. Makes 4 servings.

Per serving: 563 calories (9% calories from fat), 36 g protein, 89 g carbohydrates, 5 g total fat (2 g saturated fat), 74 mg cholesterol, 226 mg sodium

Chicken & Apple Stir-fry

Preparation time: About 20 minutes
Cooking time: About 15 minutes

•

To balance the sweetness of this stir-fry's creamy sauce, choose crisp, tart apples such as Granny Smith or Newtown Pippin.

4 teaspoons **butter or margarine**

2 large tart **apples** (about 1 lb./455 g *total*), peeled, cored, and cut into ¼-inch-thick (6-mm-thick) slices

1 pound (455 g) **boneless, skinless chicken breast,** cut into ½- by 2-inch (1- by 5-cm) strips

1 large **onion,** finely chopped

⅔ cup (160 ml) **dry sherry or apple juice**

⅓ cup (80 ml) **half-and-half**

Melt 1 tablespoon of the butter in a wide nonstick frying pan or wok over medium heat. Add apples and stir-fry just until tender to bite (about 2 minutes). Remove apples from pan with a slotted spoon and keep warm.

Increase heat to medium-high and melt remaining 1 teaspoon butter in pan. Add chicken and stir-fry until no longer pink in center; cut to test (3 to 4 minutes). Remove chicken from pan with a slotted spoon and keep warm.

Add onion and 2 tablespoons (30 ml) of the sherry to pan; stir-fry until onion is soft (about 3 minutes). Add remaining sherry and bring to a boil; boil, stirring, for 1 minute. Add half-and-half and boil, stirring, until sauce is slightly thickened (about 2 minutes). Return apples and chicken to pan and mix gently but thoroughly. Makes 4 servings.

Per serving: 309 calories (26% calories from fat), 28 g protein, 21 g carbohydrates, 8 g total fat (4 g saturated fat), 84 mg cholesterol, 126 mg sodium

Chicken Curry in Pita Bread

Pictured on facing page
Preparation time: About 20 minutes
Cooking time: About 20 minutes

•

Like Mu Shu Sandwiches (page 39), these chicken- and vegetable-stuffed pita breads are a satisfying choice for lunch or supper. The filling gets its appealing tangy-sweet flavor from yogurt, raisins, and apricot jam. When you add the yogurt, be sure to reduce the heat and stir gently and constantly; if the mixture is allowed to boil, it will curdle.

- ½ cup (75 g) raisins or dried currants
- 1 cup (240 ml) plain nonfat yogurt
- 2 tablespoons cornstarch
- 2 teaspoons olive oil
- 12 ounces (340 g) boneless, skinless chicken breast, cut into ½-inch (1-cm) pieces
- 1 medium-size onion, chopped
- 2 cloves garlic, minced or pressed
- 2 teaspoons curry powder
- ½ cup (160 g) apricot jam or preserves
  Salt and pepper
- 1 medium-size cucumber (about 8 oz./230 g), very thinly sliced
- 4 pita breads (*each* about 6 inches/15 cm in diameter), cut crosswise into halves

In a small bowl, combine raisins and ¼ cup (60 ml) water; let stand until raisins are softened (about 10 minutes), stirring occasionally. Meanwhile, in another small bowl, stir together yogurt and cornstarch until smoothly blended; set aside.

Heat oil in a wide nonstick frying pan or wok over medium-high heat. When oil is hot, add chicken and 1 tablespoon (15 ml) water. Stir-fry until meat is no longer pink in center; cut to test (3 to 4 minutes). Remove chicken from pan with a slotted spoon and keep warm. Discard drippings from pan.

Add onion, garlic, curry powder, and ¼ cup (60 ml) water to pan; stir-fry until onion is soft (about 4 minutes; do not scorch). Add water, 1 tablespoon (15 ml) at a time,

if pan appears dry. Add raisins (and soaking water) and jam. Bring to a boil; then boil, stirring, until almost all liquid has evaporated (5 to 7 minutes). Reduce heat to medium-low; stir in chicken and yogurt mixture. Simmer gently, stirring constantly, until sauce is slightly thickened (do not boil). Season to taste with salt and pepper.

To serve, divide cucumber slices equally among bread halves; fill equally with chicken mixture. Makes 4 servings.

Per serving: 506 calories (8% calories from fat), 30 g protein, 88 g carbohydrates, 5 g total fat (0.8 g saturated fat), 50 mg cholesterol, 442 mg sodium

Peanut Chicken with Rice

Preparation time: About15 minutes
Cooking time: About 25 minutes

•

What goes into a grade-school lunch box—and into a savory stir-fry sauce? Peanut butter and jam! Just a few tablespoons of each give this dish a great, slightly sweet peanut taste that both children and adults will enjoy. For refreshing contrast, squeeze a little lemon juice over the chicken and sauce.

- 1 cup (185 g) long-grain white rice
- 1 package (about 10 oz./285 g) frozen tiny peas, thawed and drained
  Cooking Sauce (recipe follows)
- 2 teaspoons Ginger Oil, page 69 (or 2 teaspoons salad oil mixed with ¼ teaspoon ground ginger)
- 1 pound (455 g) boneless, skinless chicken breast, cut into ¾-inch (2-cm) pieces
- 2 tablespoons sliced green onion
  Lemon wedges

In a 3- to 4-quart (2.8- to 3.8-liter) pan, bring 2 cups (470 ml) water to a boil over high heat; stir in rice. Reduce

Continued on page 36

Bright colors, spicy-sweet flavors, and a touch of golden curry explain the appeal of raisin-studded Chicken Curry in Pita Bread (recipe at left). Thinly sliced cucumber adds freshness and crunch.

Peanut Chicken with Rice (continued)

heat, cover, and simmer until liquid has been absorbed and rice is tender to bite (about 20 minutes). Stir peas into rice; remove from heat and keep warm. Fluff occasionally with a fork. While rice is cooking, prepare Cooking Sauce and set aside.

Heat oil in a wide nonstick frying pan or wok over medium-high heat. When oil is hot, add chicken and stir-fry until no longer pink in center; cut to test (4 to 6 minutes). Remove chicken from pan with a slotted spoon and keep warm. Discard drippings from pan and wipe pan clean (be careful; pan is hot).

Stir Cooking Sauce well and pour into pan. Stir over medium heat just until smoothly blended and heated through. Add chicken and onion; remove pan from heat and stir to coat chicken and onion with sauce.

Spoon rice mixture onto a rimmed platter and top with chicken mixture. Offer lemon wedges to squeeze over stir-fry to taste. Makes 4 servings.

Cooking Sauce. In a small bowl, stir together 3 tablespoons (45 ml) **crunchy or smooth peanut butter**, 3 tablespoons (45 ml) **plum jam** or grape jelly, 2 tablespoons (30 ml) **water**, 1½ teaspoons *each* **lemon juice** and **reduced-sodium soy sauce,** and 1 teaspoon **Oriental sesame oil.**

Per serving: 481 calories (21% calories from fat), 36 g protein, 58 g carbohydrates, 11 g total fat (2 g saturated fat), 66 mg cholesterol, 312 mg sodium

Salsa Chicken

Preparation time: About 20 minutes
Cooking time: About 10 minutes

●

A main-dish salad? A tostada without the crisp-fried tortilla? You could describe this dish either way. Cornmeal-

crusted chicken chunks, topped with warm homemade salsa and sour cream, are served on a cool, crunchy bed of shredded lettuce. On the side, you might offer low-fat tortilla chips and an orange-and-onion salad.

> Tomato Salsa (recipe follows)
> **About 8 cups (about 8 oz./230 g) finely shredded iceberg lettuce**
> 2 **large egg whites**
> ½ **cup (69 g) yellow cornmeal**
> 1½ **teaspoons chili powder**
> ½ **teaspoon ground cumin**
> 1 **pound (455 g) boneless, skinless chicken breast, cut into 1-inch (2.5-cm) pieces**
> 2 **teaspoons olive oil or salad oil**
> ½ **cup (120 ml) nonfat sour cream**
> **Cilantro sprigs**

Prepare Tomato Salsa and set aside. Divide lettuce among 4 individual plates; cover and set aside.

In a shallow bowl, beat egg whites to blend; set aside. In a large bowl, combine cornmeal, chili powder, and cumin. Add chicken and turn to coat. Then lift chicken from bowl, shaking off excess coating. Dip chicken into egg whites, then coat again with remaining cornmeal mixture.

Heat oil in a wide nonstick frying pan or wok over medium-high heat. When oil is hot, add chicken and stir-fry gently until no longer pink in center; cut to test (5 to 7 minutes). Remove from pan and keep warm. Pour Tomato Salsa into pan; reduce heat to medium and cook, stirring, until salsa is heated through and slightly thickened (1 to 2 minutes).

Arrange chicken over lettuce; top with salsa and sour cream. Garnish with cilantro sprigs. Makes 4 servings.

Tomato Salsa. In a large bowl, combine 2 medium-size **tomatoes** (about 12 oz./340 g *total*), chopped and drained well; ¼ cup (25 g) thinly sliced **green onions;** ¼ cup (60 ml) **lime juice;** 1 small **fresh jalapeño chile,** seeded and finely chopped; 1 tablespoon chopped **cilantro;** and 1 clove **garlic,** minced or pressed. If made ahead, cover and refrigerate for up to 3 hours.

Per serving: 284 calories (15% calories from fat), 34 g protein, 26 g carbohydrates, 5 g total fat (0.8 g saturated fat), 66 mg cholesterol, 152 mg sodium

Kung Pao Chicken

Preparation time: About 25 minutes
Cooking time: About 25 minutes

•

Chicken chunks and snow peas are cloaked in a highly seasoned sauce, then lightly sprinkled with peanuts.

- 1 cup (185 g) long-grain white rice

  Cooking Sauce (recipe follows)
- 1½ cups (115 g) Chinese pea pods (also called snow or sugar peas) or sugar snap peas, ends and strings removed
- 1 tablespoon cornstarch
- 1 tablespoon (15 ml) dry white wine
- ½ teaspoon sugar
- 1 pound (455 g) boneless, skinless chicken breast, cut into ¾-inch (2-cm) chunks
- 2 cloves garlic, minced or pressed
- 1 cup (130 g) peeled, shredded jicama
- 2 tablespoons salted roasted peanuts, chopped

In a 3- to 4-quart (2.8- to 3.8-liter) pan, bring 2 cups (470 ml) water to a boil over high heat; stir in rice. Reduce heat, cover, and simmer until liquid has been absorbed and rice is tender to bite (about 20 minutes). Meanwhile, prepare Cooking Sauce; set aside. Cut pea pods diagonally into ¾-inch (2-cm) pieces; set aside.

In a large bowl, dissolve cornstarch in wine; stir in sugar. Add chicken and stir to coat. Then turn chicken mixture into a wide nonstick frying pan or wok; add garlic and 1 tablespoon (15 ml) water. Stir-fry over medium-high heat until meat is no longer pink in center; cut to test (4 to 6 minutes). Remove from pan with a slotted spoon and keep warm. Add pea pods, jicama, and 1 tablespoon (15 ml) water to pan; stir-fry until pea pods are tender-crisp to bite (about 1 minute). Stir Cooking Sauce well; pour into pan and bring to a boil. Remove from heat and stir in chicken.

Spoon rice onto a rimmed platter; top with chicken mixture and sprinkle with peanuts. Makes 4 servings.

Cooking Sauce. Mix 1 tablespoon *each* **sugar** and **chili paste with garlic;** 1 tablespoon (15 ml) **unseasoned rice vinegar** or distilled white vinegar; and 1 tablespoon (15 ml) *each* **hoisin sauce** and **Oriental sesame oil.**

Per serving: 431 calories (18% calories from fat), 33 g protein, 53 g carbohydrates, 9 g total fat (1 g saturated fat), 66 mg cholesterol, 249 mg sodium

Pasta with Stir-fried Chicken & Prosciutto

Preparation time: About 10 minutes
Cooking time: About 15 minutes

•

Dijon mustard, basil, and a touch of prosciutto flavor a hearty stir-fry to serve over spinach pasta.

- ½ cup (120 ml) fat-free reduced-sodium chicken broth or dry white wine
- ¼ cup (60 ml) Dijon mustard
- 2 tablespoons (30 ml) lemon juice
- 1 teaspoon dried basil
- 8 ounces (230 g) dried spinach spaghetti
- 2 teaspoons olive oil
- 4 green onions, thinly sliced
- 2 cloves garlic, minced or pressed
- 1 ounce (30 g) prosciutto, cut into thin strips
- 1 pound (455 g) boneless, skinless chicken breast, cut into ½- by 2-inch (1- by 5-cm) strips

In a small bowl, stir together broth, mustard, lemon juice, and basil. Set aside.

In a 4- to 5-quart (3.8- to 5-liter) pan, cook spaghetti in about 8 cups (1.9 liters) boiling water until just tender to bite (8 to 10 minutes); or cook according to package directions.

Meanwhile, heat oil in a wide nonstick frying pan or wok over medium heat. When oil is hot, add onions, garlic, and prosciutto; stir-fry until prosciutto is lightly browned (about 3 minutes). Increase heat to medium-high. Add chicken and stir-fry until no longer pink in center; cut to test (3 to 4 minutes). Add broth mixture to pan and bring to a boil. Remove from heat.

Drain pasta well and place in a warm wide bowl; spoon chicken mixture over pasta. Makes 4 servings.

Per serving: 402 calories (15% calories from fat), 37 g protein, 47 g carbohydrates, 7 g total fat (1 g saturated fat), 72 mg cholesterol, 760 mg sodium

Mu Shu Sandwiches

Preparation time: About 10 minutes
Cooking time: About 10 minutes

•

Quick and easy! To make this dinner, fill pita bread halves with a simple stir-fry of chicken breast, onions, and bell peppers in hoisin sauce. If you like, dress up the sandwiches with pickled scallions and pickled sliced ginger; both are available in the Asian foods section of most supermarkets.

- 1 tablespoon (15 ml) salad oil
- 3 cups (345 g) thinly sliced onions
- 2 cups (160 g) thinly sliced green or red bell peppers
- 1 pound (455 g) boneless, skinless chicken breast, cut into ½- by 2-inch (1- by 5-cm) strips
- ¼ cup (60 ml) hoisin sauce
  Whole green onions (ends trimmed)
- 4 pita breads (*each* about 6 inches/15 cm in diameter), cut crosswise into halves
  Pickled scallions and pickled sliced ginger (optional)

Heat 2 teaspoons of the oil in a wide nonstick frying pan or wok over medium-high heat. When oil is hot, add sliced onions and bell peppers; stir-fry until vegetables are lightly browned (2 to 3 minutes). Remove vegetables from pan with a slotted spoon and keep warm.

Heat remaining 1 teaspoon oil in pan. When oil is hot, add chicken and stir-fry until no longer pink in center; cut to test (3 to 4 minutes). Add hoisin sauce to pan; then return vegetables to pan and stir to mix well. Pour into a bowl and garnish with green onions. Fill bread halves with chicken mixture and, if desired, pickled scallions and pickled ginger. Makes 4 servings.

. . . .

Quick-cooked strips of turkey breast are cloaked in a vivid fruit sauce to make tempting Raspberry-glazed Turkey Sauté (recipe at right). Served over tender green fettuccine, the dish is garnished with tarragon sprigs and sprinkled with juicy ripe raspberries.

Per serving: 401 calories (14% calories from fat), 34 g protein, 52 g carbohydrates, 6 g total fat (1 g saturated fat), 66 mg cholesterol, 910 mg sodium

Raspberry-glazed Turkey Sauté

Pictured on facing page
Preparation time: About 20 minutes
Cooking time: About 15 minutes

•

Poultry and fruit are classic partners: witness the traditional pairing of roast turkey with cranberry sauce. Here, turkey tenderloin joins up with sweet red raspberries. You toss thin strips of meat with a sauce of raspberry vinegar and jam, then top the finished dish with ripe whole berries. (When fresh raspberries are unavailable or unaffordable, use 1 cup of orange segments instead.)

- 3 green onions
- ⅓ cup (100 g) seedless red raspberry jam or jelly
- 3 tablespoons (45 ml) raspberry or red wine vinegar
- 1 tablespoon Dijon mustard
- ½ teaspoon grated orange peel
- ¾ teaspoon chopped fresh tarragon or ¼ teaspoon dried tarragon
- 8 ounces (230 g) dried eggless spinach fettuccine or plain fettuccine
- 1 teaspoon olive oil or salad oil
- 2 turkey breast tenderloins (about 1 lb./455 g *total*), cut into ¼- by 2-inch (6-mm by 5-cm) strips
  About 1 cup (123 g) fresh raspberries
  Tarragon sprigs

Trim and discard ends of onions. Cut onions into 2-inch (5-cm) lengths; then cut each piece lengthwise into slivers. Set aside. In a small bowl, stir together jam, vinegar, mustard, orange peel, and chopped tarragon; set aside.

In a 4- to 5-quart (3.8- to 5-liter) pan, cook fettuccine in about 8 cups (1.9 liters) boiling water until just tender to bite (8 to 10 minutes); or cook according to package directions.

Meanwhile, heat oil in a wide nonstick frying pan or wok over medium-high heat. When oil is hot, add turkey

Continued on next page

Raspberry-glazed Turkey Sauté (continued)

and 1 tablespoon (15 ml) water. Stir-fry just until turkey is no longer pink in center; cut to test (about 2 minutes). Add water, 1 tablespoon (15 ml) at a time, if pan appears dry. Remove turkey from pan with a slotted spoon and keep warm. Discard drippings from pan; wipe pan clean (be careful; pan is hot).

Add jam mixture to pan and bring to a boil over medium-high heat; then boil, stirring, just until jam is melted and sauce is smooth (about 1 minute). Remove from heat and stir in turkey and onions.

Drain pasta well and divide among 4 warm individual rimmed plates or shallow bowls; top with turkey mixture. Sprinkle with raspberries and garnish with tarragon sprigs. Makes 4 servings.

Per serving: 436 calories (7% calories from fat), 36 g protein, 65 g carbohydrates, 3 g total fat (0.5 g saturated fat), 70 mg cholesterol, 201 mg sodium

Brunch Paella

Preparation time: About 15 minutes
Cooking time: 35 to 40 minutes

•

This super company dish is sure to satisfy hearty appetites at brunch or supper. To make it, use turkey Italian sausage—mild for a tamer paella, spicy-hot if you want to start (or end) the day with a bang.

  1 pound (455 g) turkey Italian sausages (casings removed), crumbled into ½-inch (1-cm) pieces
  1 cup (185 g) long-grain white rice
  1 large onion, chopped
  2 cloves garlic, minced or pressed
  2 cups (470 ml) fat-free reduced-sodium chicken broth
1½ cups (235 g) chopped tomatoes
  ¼ teaspoon saffron threads
  1 package (about 9 oz./255 g) frozen artichoke hearts, thawed and drained
  ¼ cup (15 g) chopped parsley
     Lemon wedges

In a wide nonstick frying pan or wok, stir-fry sausage over medium-high heat until browned (7 to 10 minutes).

Remove sausage from pan with a slotted spoon; set aside. Pour off and discard all but 1 teaspoon fat from pan.

Add rice to pan; stir-fry until rice begins to turn opaque (about 3 minutes). Add onion, garlic, and 2 tablespoons (30 ml) water; stir-fry for 5 more minutes. Add more water, 1 tablespoon (15 ml) at a time, if pan appears dry. Stir in broth, tomatoes, saffron, artichokes, and parsley; then return sausage to pan. Bring to a boil; reduce heat, cover, and simmer until liquid has been absorbed and rice is tender to bite (about 20 minutes). Serve with lemon wedges. Makes 4 to 6 servings.

Per serving: 346 calories (26% calories from fat), 22 g protein, 44 g carbohydrates, 10 g total fat (3 g saturated fat), 49 mg cholesterol, 888 mg sodium

Stir-fried Curried Turkey with Coconut Rice

Preparation time: About 20 minutes
Cooking time: About 25 minutes

•

White rice cooked in low-fat milk and sweetened with a little coconut makes a superb, rich-tasting foil for this golden turkey curry.

     Coconut Rice (recipe follows)
  2 tablespoons (30 ml) lemon juice
  1 clove garlic, minced or pressed
  ½ teaspoon ground cumin
  ¼ teaspoon chili powder
  2 turkey breast tenderloins (about 1 lb./455 g *total*), cut into 1-inch (2.5-cm) pieces
  ½ cup (75 g) golden raisins
  ¼ cup (60 ml) dry white wine
  2 medium-size carrots (about 8 oz./230 g *total*), cut into ¼-inch (6-mm) slanting slices
  1 large onion, thinly sliced
  2 teaspoons olive oil or salad oil
  2 to 3 teaspoons curry powder
  1 to 2 tablespoons chopped fresh mint or parsley
  2 tablespoons salted roasted cashews, chopped
     Mint or parsley sprigs

Prepare Coconut Rice. Meanwhile, in a large bowl, combine 1 tablespoon (15 ml) water, lemon juice, garlic, cumin, and chili powder. Add turkey and stir to coat. Set aside; stir occasionally. In a small bowl, combine raisins and wine; let stand until raisins are softened (about 10 minutes), stirring occasionally.

In a wide nonstick frying pan or wok, combine carrots, onion, and ¼ cup (60 ml) water. Cover and cook over medium-high heat until carrots are tender-crisp to bite (about 5 minutes). Uncover and stir-fry until liquid has evaporated. Remove vegetables from pan with a slotted spoon and keep warm.

Heat oil in pan. When oil is hot, add turkey mixture. Stir-fry just until meat is no longer pink in center; cut to test (3 to 4 minutes). Add water, 1 tablespoon (15 ml) at a time, if pan appears dry. Add curry powder and stir-fry just until fragrant (about 30 seconds; do not scorch).

Add raisins (and soaking liquid) to pan; return vegetables to pan. Bring to a boil; then boil, stirring, until liquid has evaporated (about 2 minutes). Remove from heat; stir in chopped mint and cashews. Spoon Coconut Rice into 4 wide bowls; top with turkey mixture and garnish with mint sprigs. Makes 4 servings.

Coconut Rice. In a 3- to 4-quart (2.8- to 3.8-liter) pan, combine 1 cup (240 ml) *each* **water** and **low-fat milk.** Bring just to a boil over medium-high heat. Stir in 1 cup (185 g) **long-grain white rice.** Reduce heat, cover, and simmer until liquid has been absorbed and rice is tender to bite (about 20 minutes). Stir in ¼ cup (20 g) **sweetened shredded coconut.** Keep warm until ready to serve, fluffing occasionally with a fork.

Per serving: 502 calories (13% calories from fat), 36 g protein, 70 g carbohydrates, 7 g total fat (2 g saturated fat), 72 mg cholesterol, 158 mg sodium

Stir-fried Turkey Fajitas

Preparation time: About 10 minutes
Cooking time: About 15 minutes

•

A marinade of lime juice and balsamic vinegar imparts a wonderful flavor to this lean stir-fry of turkey strips, red onion, and green bell pepper.

　　Lime Marinade (page 42)
2　**turkey breast tenderloins (about 1 lb./455 g** *total***), cut into ½- by 2-inch (1- by 5-cm) strips**
4　**low-fat flour tortillas (***each* **7 to 9 inches/18 to 23 cm in diameter)**
1　**tablespoon (15 ml) olive oil**
1　**large green bell pepper (about 8 oz./230 g), seeded and cut into thin strips**
1　**large red onion, thinly sliced**
　　Lime wedges

Prepare Lime Marinade. Add turkey and stir to coat. Set aside; stir occasionally.

Brush tortillas lightly with hot water; then stack tortillas, wrap in foil, and heat in a 350°F/175°C oven until warm (10 to 12 minutes).

Meanwhile, heat 2 teaspoons of the oil in a wide nonstick frying pan or wok over medium-high heat. When oil is hot, add bell pepper and onion and stir-fry until vegetables are lightly browned (2 to 3 minutes). Remove vegetables from pan with a slotted spoon and keep warm.

Heat remaining 1 teaspoon oil in pan. When oil is hot, lift turkey from marinade and drain briefly (reserve marinade). Add turkey to pan and stir-fry until no longer pink in center; cut to test (2 to 3 minutes). Add marinade and bring to a boil; return vegetables to pan and mix gently. Spoon mixture onto a platter.

Offer tortillas and lime wedges alongside turkey mixture. To eat, fill tortillas with turkey mixture; add a squeeze of lime, roll up, and eat out of hand. Makes 4 servings.

Continued on next page

Stir-fried Turkey Fajitas (contin-

Lime Marinade. In a large bowl, stir together ¼ cup (60 ml) **lime juice**, 1 tablespoon (15 ml) **balsamic or red wine vinegar**, 1 clove **garlic** (minced or pressed), and ½ teaspoon *each* **ground coriander, ground cumin,** and **honey.**

Per serving: 280 calories (21% calories from fat), 31 g protein, 23 g carbohydrates, 6 g total fat (0.7 g saturated fat), 71 mg cholesterol, 356 mg sodium

Turkey with Penne, Feta & Sun-dried Tomatoes

Pictured on facing page
Preparation time: About 15 minutes
Cooking time: About 15 minutes

•

If you're eating light but can't do without cheese, try sticking to the sharper, tangier types—the stronger the flavor, the less you'll need to use. Here, just 2 ounces of feta add zest to a hearty turkey-and-pasta supper dish.

- 2 to 4 tablespoons (15 to 30 g) sun-dried tomatoes in olive oil
- Cooking Sauce (recipe follows)
- 1 small onion
- 8 ounces (230 g) dried penne or ziti
- 2 turkey breast tenderloins (about 1 lb./455 g *total*), cut into ½-inch (1-cm) pieces
- 1½ teaspoons chopped fresh oregano or ½ teaspoon dried oregano
- 1 large tomato (about 8 oz./230 g), chopped and drained well
- 2 tablespoons drained capers
- ½ cup (65 g) crumbled feta cheese
- Oregano sprigs

Drain sun-dried tomatoes well (reserve oil) and pat dry with paper towels. Then chop tomatoes and set aside. Prepare Cooking Sauce and set aside. Cut onion in half lengthwise; then cut each half crosswise into thin slices. Set aside.

In a 4- to 5-quart (3.8- to 5-liter) pan, cook penne in about 8 cups (1.9 liters) boiling water until just tender to bite (8 to 10 minutes); or cook according to package directions. Drain pasta well and transfer to a warm large bowl; keep warm.

While pasta is cooking, measure 2 teaspoons of the oil from sun-dried tomatoes. Heat oil in a wide nonstick frying pan or wok over medium-high heat. When oil is hot, add turkey and chopped oregano. Stir-fry just until meat is no longer pink in center; cut to test (2 to 3 minutes). Add water, 1 tablespoon (15 ml) at a time, if pan appears dry. Remove turkey from pan with a slotted spoon; transfer to bowl with pasta and keep warm.

Add sun-dried tomatoes and onion to pan; stir-fry until onion is soft (about 4 minutes). Add water, 1 tablespoon (15 ml) at a time, if pan appears dry. Stir Cooking Sauce well and pour into pan. Cook, stirring, until sauce boils and thickens slightly (1 to 2 minutes). Remove from heat and stir in fresh tomato and capers. Spoon tomato mixture over pasta and turkey; mix gently but thoroughly.

Divide turkey mixture among 4 warm individual rimmed plates or shallow bowls. Sprinkle with cheese and garnish with oregano sprigs. Makes 4 servings.

Cooking Sauce. In a small bowl, stir together ½ cup (120 ml) **fat-free reduced-sodium chicken broth**, 2 tablespoons (30 ml) **dry white wine**, and 1 teaspoon **cornstarch** until blended.

Per serving: 489 calories (24% calories from fat), 39 g protein, 52 g carbohydrates, 13 g total fat (4 g saturated fat), 83 mg cholesterol, 462 mg sodium

••

When this dish is on the menu, rave reviews are bound to follow. Turkey with Penne, Feta & Sun-dried Tomatoes (recipe at left) combines two all-time favorites—pasta and poultry—in a light sauce featuring both fresh and sun-dried tomatoes.

Turkey Stir-fry by the Numbers

Stir-fries are generally simple dishes: bite-size pieces of meat, poultry, or fish, sliced vegetables, and a light sauce to meld all the flavors. But when you don't have a recipe to follow, figuring out the correct proportions of ingredients can be somewhat tricky. To help you with this problem, we devised the chart at right below; it lists the amounts to use for a perfect two-, four-, or six-serving turkey stir-fry.

To make the cooking process especially fast, we start with leftover cooked turkey or other meat. You can choose from a variety of vegetables; for a good balance of flavor and texture, use three or four different kinds. If you're really short on time, you can turn to the precut fresh vegetables available at most supermarkets. Be aware, though, that these are sometimes drier than freshly cut vegetables.

Unusual and delicious combinations that go well with turkey include: Japanese eggplant, onions, Chinese pea pods, and carrots; yams, bell peppers, and fresh button mushrooms; onions, broccoli, and mustard greens; zucchini, yellow bell peppers, onions, and enoki mushrooms; and red onions, green beans, and dried cranberries.

Our spicy cooking sauce nicely complements whatever meat and vegetables you use. If you plan to serve the stir-fry over hot rice or pasta, it's a good idea to double the sauce, since the rice or pasta will absorb much of it. (You can assemble the sauce ahead and refrigerate it for up to 2 days.)

Cooking Sauce. In a small bowl, stir together ⅓ cup (80 ml) **fat-free reduced-sodium chicken broth**; ⅓ cup (80 ml) **mirin** or cream sherry; ¼ cup (60 ml) **reduced-sodium soy sauce**; 3 tablespoons minced **fresh ginger**; 3 cloves **garlic**, minced or pressed; 1 tablespoon **cornstarch**; and 2 teaspoons **Oriental sesame oil**. Makes about 1 cup.

Cooking directions. Follow the steps below to prepare your stir-fry, referring to the amounts shown in the chart.

1. Prepare Cooking Sauce (above). Set aside.

2. Heat oil in a wide nonstick frying pan or wok over medium-high heat. When oil is hot, add your choice of cut-up fresh vegetables.

3. Stir-fry until vegetables are hot and bright in color; vegetables may begin to brown (about 2 minutes).

4. Add broth (if using chicken broth, use the fat-free reduced-sodium type). Cover and cook until vegetables are just tender to bite (2 to 6 minutes). Uncover; stir-fry until liquid has evaporated.

5. Stir Cooking Sauce well; pour into pan, then add turkey. Bring to a boil, stirring. Stir in your choice of additions and cook until all ingredients are heated through (30 seconds to 2 minutes).

6. Spoon stir-fry onto a platter; sprinkle with a topping, if desired. Serve with rice, pasta, or napa cabbage.

Stir-fry Proportions & Choices

INGREDIENTS	SERVES 2	SERVES 4	SERVES 6
Cooking oil Olive or vegetable	2 tsp.	1 tbsp.	1½ tbsp.
Vegetables Broccoli flowerets, bell pepper wedges (green, red, or yellow), sliced carrots, green beans (cut into 1½-inch pieces), sliced Japanese eggplant, onion wedges, sliced mushrooms (button or shiitake), yams (peeled and thinly sliced), or sliced zucchini	3 cups	5 cups	7 cups
Broth or water	¼ cup	⅓ cup	½ cup
Cooking Sauce (above)	½ cup	¾ cup	1 cup
Cooked turkey or meat Cut into bite-size pieces	1 cup	2 cups	3 cups
Additions Anaheim or pasilla chiles (sliced and seeded), Chinese pea pods (ends and strings removed), mustard greens, or kale or red cabbage (thinly sliced)	Vary amounts to personal taste		
Toppings Dried cranberries, pitted calamata or green olives, crushed red pepper flakes, or enoki mushrooms	Vary amounts to personal taste		
On the side Cooked white or brown rice or noodles; or uncooked, thinly sliced napa cabbage	2 cups	4 cups	6 cups

Mediterranean Turkey with Herbed Couscous

Preparation time: About 15 minutes
Cooking time: About 10 minutes

●

Oregano, lemon, and pungent Greek olives give this dish its Mediterranean flavor. Start by cooking the couscous; then prepare a garlicky stir-fry of turkey and red bell pepper strips to serve alongside.

- 2 turkey breast tenderloins (about 1 lb./455 g *total*), cut into ½-inch (1-cm) pieces
- 2 cloves garlic, minced or pressed
- 1 teaspoon paprika
- ½ teaspoon grated lemon peel
- ⅛ teaspoon salt (optional)
- ⅛ teaspoon pepper
   Cooking Sauce (recipe follows)
- 1 cup (240 ml) fat-free reduced-sodium chicken broth
- ⅔ cup (160 ml) low-fat milk
- 1½ teaspoons chopped fresh oregano or ½ teaspoon dried oregano
- 1 cup (185 g) couscous
- 1 medium-size red bell pepper (about 6 oz./170 g), seeded and cut into thin strips
- 2 teaspoons olive oil
- ⅓ to ½ cup (45 to 70 g) chopped pitted calamata olives
- ¼ cup (15 g) finely chopped parsley
   Oregano sprigs

In a large bowl, mix turkey, garlic, paprika, ¼ teaspoon of the lemon peel, salt (if used), and pepper; set aside. Prepare Cooking Sauce and set aside.

In a 3- to 4-quart (2.8- to 3.8-liter) pan, combine broth, milk, chopped oregano, and remaining ¼ teaspoon lemon peel. Bring just to a boil over medium-high heat; stir in couscous. Cover, remove from heat, and let stand until liquid has been absorbed (about 5 minutes). Transfer to a rimmed platter and keep warm; fluff occasionally with a fork.

While couscous is standing, in a wide nonstick frying pan or wok, combine bell pepper and 2 tablespoons (30 ml) water. Stir-fry over medium-high heat until pepper is just tender-crisp to bite (about 2 minutes); add water, 1 tablespoon (15 ml) at a time, if pan appears dry. Remove from pan with a slotted spoon and keep warm.

Heat oil in pan. When oil is hot, add turkey mixture and stir-fry just until meat is no longer pink in center; cut to test (2 to 3 minutes). Stir Cooking Sauce well; pour into pan. Then add bell pepper and olives; cook, stirring, until sauce boils and thickens slightly (1 to 2 minutes). Pour turkey mixture over couscous. Sprinkle with parsley and garnish with oregano sprigs. Makes 4 servings.

Cooking Sauce. In a bowl, smoothly blend 2 teaspoons **cornstarch** with 2 tablespoons (30 ml) **balsamic vinegar.** Stir in ½ cup (120 ml) **fat-free reduced-sodium chicken broth.**

Per serving: 412 calories (20% calories from fat), 37 g protein, 44 g carbohydrates, 9 g total fat (1 g saturated fat), 71 mg cholesterol, 823 mg sodium

Seafood Dishes

Delicate and naturally lean, seafood is a top choice for healthful eating. In this chapter, we've combined fish and shellfish with fresh fruits and vegetables, tender pasta and grains, and imaginative sauces to make dishes both family and guests will enjoy.

....

Simple, refreshingly light Scallop & Pea Pod Stir-fry with Papaya (recipe on page 48) is a tantalizing meal in an edible bowl. To make the dish, spoon the ginger-sauced shellfish and crisp snow peas into sweet, ripe papaya halves.

Scallop & Pea Pod Stir-fry with Papaya

Pictured on page 46
Preparation time: About 15 minutes
Cooking time: About 8 minutes

●

Colorful, fragrant, and just plain delicious, this dish is a winner. Be prepared—it's likely to disappear almost as soon as you bring the platter to the table.

    Ginger Sauce (recipe follows)
2 medium-size papayas (about 1 lb./455 g *each*)
1 pound (455 g) sea scallops
1 tablespoon butter or margarine
1½ cups (115 g) fresh Chinese pea pods (also called snow or sugar peas) or sugar snap peas, ends and strings removed; or 1 package (about 6 oz./170 g) frozen Chinese pea pods, thawed and drained

Prepare Ginger Sauce and set aside. Cut unpeeled papayas lengthwise into halves; remove and discard seeds. Set papaya halves, cut side up, on a platter; cover and set aside.

   Rinse scallops and pat dry; cut into bite-size pieces, if desired. Melt butter in a wide nonstick frying pan or wok over medium-high heat. Add scallops and fresh pea pods (if using frozen pea pods, add later, as directed below). Stir-fry until scallops are just opaque in center; cut to test (3 to 4 minutes). Stir Ginger Sauce well, then pour into pan. Stir in frozen pea pods, if using. Cook, stirring, until sauce boils and thickens slightly (1 to 2 minutes). Spoon scallop mixture equally into papaya halves. Makes 4 servings.

Ginger Sauce. In a small bowl, stir together 2 teaspoons **cornstarch** and ¼ cup (60 ml) **water** until blended. Then stir in 1 tablespoon (15 ml) *each* **honey** and **lemon juice,** ½ teaspoon **ground ginger,** and ½ teaspoon **Chinese five-spice** (or ⅛ teaspoon *each* anise seeds, ground all-spice, ground cinnamon, and ground cloves).

Per serving: 220 calories (16% calories from fat), 21 g protein, 26 g carbohydrates, 4 g total fat (2 g saturated fat), 45 mg cholesterol, 219 mg sodium

Scallop Scampi

Preparation time: About 15 minutes
Cooking time: About 15 minutes

●

In Italy, *scampi* just means shrimp. In America, though, the word usually refers to shrimp prepared a certain way: sautéed with plenty of oil, butter, and garlic. In making this scampi-inspired scallop dish, we've been generous with the garlic—there are three cloves in the stir-fry, another in the crisp crumb topping—but we've cut the fat to a single tablespoon. The result? A great-tasting dish that's lean, too.

    Stir-fried Crumbs (recipe follows)
1 tablespoon chopped parsley
2 tablespoons (30 ml) dry white wine
1 teaspoon lemon juice
½ teaspoon honey
1 bunch watercress (about 5 oz./140 g), coarse stems removed, sprigs rinsed and crisped
1 pound (455 g) sea scallops
1½ teaspoons butter or margarine
1½ teaspoons olive oil
3 cloves garlic, minced or pressed
    Lemon wedges

Prepare Stir-fried Crumbs; let cool slightly. Stir parsley into crumbs and set aside. In a small bowl, stir together wine, lemon juice, and honey; set aside. Arrange watercress on a large rimmed platter; cover and set aside.

   Rinse scallops and pat dry; cut into bite-size pieces, if desired. Melt butter in oil in a wide nonstick frying pan or wok over medium-high heat. When butter mixture is hot, add garlic, 1 tablespoon (15 ml) water, and scallops. Stir-fry until scallops are just opaque in center; cut to test (3 to 4 minutes).

   Stir wine mixture well and pour into pan; bring just to a boil. With a slotted spoon, lift scallops from pan; arrange over watercress. Pour pan juices into a small pitcher. Sprinkle scallops with Stir-fried Crumbs and garnish with lemon wedges. Offer pan juices to add to taste. Makes 4 servings.

Stir-fried Crumbs. Tear 1 slice (about 1 oz./30 g) **sour-dough sandwich bread** into pieces; whirl in a blender or food processor to make fine crumbs. In a wide non-stick frying pan or wok, combine crumbs, 1½ teaspoons **water,** ½ teaspoon **olive oil,** and 1 clove **garlic,** minced or pressed. Stir-fry over medium heat until crumbs are crisp and golden (about 5 minutes); remove from pan and set aside. If made ahead, let cool; then cover airtight and store at room temperature until next day.

Per serving: 168 calories (27% calories from fat), 21 g protein, 9 g carbohydrates, 5 g total fat (1 g saturated fat), 41 mg cholesterol, 257 mg sodium

Shrimp Sauté

Preparation time: About 15 minutes
Cooking time: About 25 minutes

Big shrimp in a simple vegetable-wine sauce are delightful for family meals or casual company gatherings. Serve with steamed broccoli or asparagus and a crusty loaf of French bread.

-   2 teaspoons butter or margarine
-   ½ cup (60 g) finely chopped celery
-   ⅓ cup (40 g) finely chopped shallots
-   2 cloves garlic, minced or pressed
-   1 medium-size red bell pepper (about 6 oz./170 g), seeded and finely chopped
-   1¼ cups (300 ml) fat-free reduced-sodium chicken broth
-   1 pound (455 g) large raw shrimp (31 to 35 per lb.), shelled and deveined
-   ⅔ cup (160 ml) fruity white wine, such as Johannisberg Riesling

Melt butter in a wide nonstick frying pan or wok over medium-high heat. Add celery, shallots, garlic, bell pepper, and broth. Cook, stirring often, until liquid has evaporated (about 10 minutes).

Add shrimp to pan and stir-fry until just opaque in center; cut to test (3 to 4 minutes). Remove shrimp from pan with tongs or a slotted spoon; place in a shallow serving bowl and keep warm. Add wine to pan and bring to a boil; then boil, stirring often, until liquid is

reduced by about two-thirds (about 7 minutes). Spoon sauce over shrimp. Makes 4 servings.

Per serving: 140 calories (23% calories from fat), 20 g protein, 6 g carbohydrates, 4 g total fat (2 g saturated fat), 145 mg cholesterol, 374 mg sodium

Coriander-Curry Shrimp

Preparation time: About 15 minutes
Cooking time: About 15 minutes

Shrimp and coconut taste delicious together—and the flavor gets even better when you add pineapple and curry. Serve this mildly spicy stir-fry over vermicelli, perhaps with a selection of tropical fruits on the side.

-   12 ounces to 1 pound (340 to 455 g) dried vermicelli or spaghetti
-   2 teaspoons cornstarch
-   ⅔ cup (160 ml) pineapple-coconut juice (or ⅔ cup/160 ml unsweetened pineapple juice plus ¼ cup/20 g sweetened shredded coconut)
-   1 teaspoon salad oil
-   1 large onion, thinly sliced
-   1 clove garlic, minced or pressed
-   1 tablespoon *each* curry powder and ground coriander
-   ¼ teaspoon ground red pepper (cayenne)
-   1½ pounds (680 g) large raw shrimp (31 to 35 per lb.), shelled and deveined
-   2 tablespoons finely chopped parsley
    Lime wedges
    Salt

In a 6- to 8-quart (6- to 8-liter) pan, cook vermicelli in about 4 quarts (3.8 liters) boiling water until just tender to bite (8 to 10 minutes); or cook according to package directions. Drain well, transfer to a warm rimmed platter, and keep warm.

While pasta is cooking, in a small bowl, stir together cornstarch and pineapple-coconut juice until blended; set aside. Heat oil in a wide nonstick frying pan or wok over medium-high heat. When oil is hot, add onion, garlic, and 2 tablespoons (30 ml) water. Stir-fry until liquid has

Continued on next page

Coriander-Curry Shrimp (continued)

has evaporated and onion is soft and beginning to brown (about 5 minutes).

Add curry powder, coriander, and red pepper to pan; stir to blend. Immediately add shrimp and stir-fry for 2 minutes. Stir cornstarch mixture well; pour into pan. Then stir until sauce is bubbly and shrimp are just opaque in center; cut to test (1 to 2 more minutes). Add parsley and mix gently but thoroughly. Spoon shrimp mixture over pasta; garnish with lime wedges. Season to taste with salt. Makes 6 servings.

Per serving: 402 calories (10% calories from fat), 28 g protein, 60 g carbohydrates, 5 g total fat (1 g saturated fat), 140 mg cholesterol, 152 mg sodium

Lemon Shrimp over Caper Couscous

Pictured on facing page
Preparation time: About 20 minutes
Cooking time: About 15 minutes

•

Add plenty of tangy flavor, and you won't miss the fat! That's the rule we've followed in this recipe. Shrimp are seasoned with lemon and garlic, then served over couscous dotted with pungent capers.

1 **pound (455 g) large raw shrimp (31 to 35 per lb.), shelled and deveined**

2 **cloves garlic, minced or pressed (optional)**

¾ **teaspoon chopped fresh oregano or ¼ teaspoon dried oregano**

½ **teaspoon grated lemon peel**

⅛ **teaspoon pepper**
    Cooking Sauce (recipe follows)

8 **ounces (230 g) asparagus**

1 **medium-size red bell pepper (about 6 oz./170 g)**

1½ **cups (360 ml) fat-free reduced-sodium chicken broth**

1 **cup (185 g) couscous**

2 **tablespoons (30 ml) seasoned rice vinegar (or 2 tablespoons/30 ml distilled white vinegar plus 1 teaspoon sugar)**

1 **to 2 tablespoons drained capers**

1 **tablespoon (15 ml) olive oil**
    Lemon wedges and oregano sprigs

In a large bowl, mix shrimp, garlic (if used), chopped oregano, ¼ teaspoon of the lemon peel, and pepper. Set aside; stir occasionally.

Prepare Cooking Sauce and set aside. Snap off and discard tough ends of asparagus; cut spears into ½-inch (1-cm) slanting slices and set aside. Seed bell pepper, cut into thin strips, and set aside.

In a 3- to 4-quart (2.8- to 3.8-liter) pan, combine broth and remaining ¼ teaspoon lemon peel. Bring to a boil over high heat; stir in couscous. Cover, remove from heat, and let stand until liquid has been absorbed (about 5 minutes). Stir in vinegar and capers. Keep couscous warm; fluff occasionally with a fork.

In a wide nonstick frying pan or wok, combine asparagus, bell pepper, and ⅓ cup (80 ml) water. Cover and cook over medium-high heat until asparagus is almost tender to bite (about 3 minutes). Uncover and stir-fry until liquid has evaporated. Remove vegetables from pan and set aside.

Heat oil in pan. When oil is hot, add shrimp mixture and stir-fry for 2 minutes. Stir Cooking Sauce well and pour into pan; then return asparagus and bell pepper to pan. Cook, stirring, until sauce boils and thickens slightly and shrimp are just opaque in center; cut to test (1 to 2 more minutes). Remove from heat.

To serve, spoon couscous onto a rimmed platter; top with shrimp mixture. Garnish with lemon wedges and oregano sprigs. Makes 4 servings.

Cooking Sauce. In a small bowl, stir together 1 tablespoon **cornstarch** and 2 tablespoons **dry sherry** until blended. Then stir in ½ cup **fat-free reduced-sodium chicken broth**.

Per serving: 355 calories (14% calories from fat), 27 g protein, 46 g carbohydrates, 5 g total fat (0.8 g saturated fat), 140 mg cholesterol, 696 mg sodium

• •

For a nutritious and great-tasting family meal, serve succulent shrimp and tender asparagus over piquant couscous. Dress up Lemon Shrimp over Caper Couscous (recipe at left) with garnishes of fresh oregano and lemon wedges.

Sauces

The three sauces on this page offer easy ways to dress up stir-fried meats, poultry, seafood—even plain vegetables. Try Cool Yogurt Sauce with salmon, beef, or tender-crisp carrots; spoon Citrus-Horseradish Cream over pork, asparagus, or broccoli. Grape Chutney, good warm or cool, is a perfect complement for lamb (see page 64) or chicken.

Grape Chutney

Pictured on page 62
Preparation time: About 10 minutes
Cooking time: About 45 minutes

•

1   large onion, finely chopped
1   large tart apple such as Newtown Pippin or McIntosh (about 8 oz./230 g), peeled, cored, and finely chopped
2   cups (320 g) seedless red or green grapes
⅓   cup (75 g) firmly packed brown sugar
⅓   cup (80 ml) red wine vinegar
⅛   teaspoon pepper
    Salt

In a wide nonstick frying pan or wok, combine onion and ¼ cup (60 ml) water. Cook over medium-high heat, stirring occasionally, until liquid evaporates and onion begins to brown and stick to pan bottom. To deglaze pan, add ¼ cup (60 ml) more water and stir to scrape browned bits free from pan bottom. Then continue to cook, stirring often, until liquid evaporates and browned bits stick to pan again. Deglaze with ¼ cup (60 ml) more water; then cook, stirring often, until onion is richly browned. (Total cooking time will be 10 to 15 minutes.)

To pan, add apple, grapes, ½ cup (120 ml) water, sugar, vinegar, and pepper. Bring to a boil; then reduce heat, cover, and simmer until grapes begin to split (about 10 minutes).

Uncover. Increase heat to medium-high and cook, stirring often, until mixture is thick and almost all liquid has evaporated (about 20 minutes); as mixture thickens, watch carefully and stir more often to prevent scorching. Season to taste with salt. If made ahead, let cool; then cover and refrigerate for up to 3 days. Reheat before serving, if desired. Makes about 2¼ cups (530 ml).

Per ¼ cup: 66 calories (2% calories from fat), 0.4 g protein, 17 g carbohydrates, 0.1 g total fat (0 g saturated fat), 0 mg cholesterol, 4 mg sodium

Cool Yogurt Sauce

Pictured on page 67
Preparation time: About 5 minutes

•

1   cup (240 ml) plain nonfat yogurt
1   tablespoon *each* chopped fresh mint and cilantro
    Salt
    Fresh mint and cilantro leaves (optional)

In a small bowl, stir together yogurt, chopped mint, and chopped cilantro. Season to taste with salt. If made ahead, cover and refrigerate for up to 4 hours; stir before serving. Sprinkle with mint and cilantro leaves just before serving, if desired. Makes about 1 cup (240 ml).

Per tablespoon: 8 calories (2% calories from fat), 0.8 g protein, 1 g carbohydrates, 0 g total fat (0 g saturated fat), 0.3 mg cholesterol, 11 mg sodium

Citrus-Horseradish Cream

Preparation time: About 5 minutes

•

1   cup (240 ml) nonfat sour cream
3   tablespoons (60 g) orange marmalade
2   teaspoons prepared horseradish
    About 1 teaspoon grated orange peel
    Honey
    Ground white pepper

In a small bowl, stir together sour cream, marmalade, horseradish, and 1 teaspoon of the orange peel until smoothly blended. Season to taste with honey and white pepper. If made ahead, cover and refrigerate until next day; stir before serving. Garnish with orange peel. Makes about 1¼ cups (300 ml).

Per tablespoon: 16 calories (0% calories from fat), 0.8 g protein, 3 g carbohydrates, 0 g total fat (0 g saturated fat), 0 mg cholesterol, 10 mg sodium

Chili Shrimp

Preparation time: About 20 minutes
Cooking time: About 25 minutes

•

East meets West in this spicy-sweet entrée. The sauce will remind you of basic barbecue, but it's accented with ginger, soy, and sesame oil.

- 1 cup (185 g) long-grain white rice
- 1 tablespoon sugar
- 3 tablespoons (45 ml) catsup
- 1 tablespoon (15 ml) *each* cider vinegar and reduced-sodium soy sauce
- ½ to 1 teaspoon crushed red pepper flakes
- 1 tablespoon (15 ml) salad oil
- 1 pound (455 g) large raw shrimp (31 to 35 per lb.), shelled (leave tails attached) and deveined
- 1 tablespoon minced fresh ginger
- 3 cloves garlic, minced or pressed
- ½ teaspoon Oriental sesame oil

  About ¼ cup (25 g) sliced green onions, or to taste

In a 3- to 4-quart (2.8- to 3.8-liter) pan, bring 2 cups (470 ml) water to a boil over high heat; stir in rice. Reduce heat, cover, and simmer until liquid has been absorbed and rice is tender to bite (about 20 minutes).

Meanwhile, in a small bowl, stir together sugar, catsup, vinegar, soy sauce, and red pepper flakes until sugar is dissolved; set aside.

Heat salad oil in a wide nonstick frying pan or wok over medium-high heat. When oil is hot, add shrimp. Stir-fry until just opaque in center; cut to test (3 to 4 minutes). Remove shrimp from pan with tongs or a slotted spoon; keep warm.

To pan, add ginger and garlic; stir-fry just until garlic is fragrant (about 30 seconds; do not scorch). Stir catsup mixture and pour into pan; bring to a boil, stirring. Remove pan from heat and add shrimp and sesame oil; mix gently but thoroughly.

Spoon rice onto a rimmed platter; spoon shrimp mixture over rice and sprinkle with onions. Makes 4 servings.

Per serving: 335 calories (16% calories from fat), 23 g protein, 46 g carbohydrates, 6 g total fat (0.9 g saturated fat), 140 mg cholesterol, 423 mg sodium

Shrimp with Parsley Pesto & Linguine

Preparation time: About 10 minutes
Cooking time: About 25 minutes

•

Ideal for any time of year, this pretty pasta entrée features plump pink shrimp and a refreshing pesto based on parsley and toasted almonds.

- ¼ cup (35 g) whole unblanched almonds
- 2 cups (120 g) lightly packed parsley sprigs
- ¼ cup (60 ml) plus 1 teaspoon olive oil
- 3 tablespoons (45 ml) white wine vinegar
- 1 clove garlic, peeled
- 1 tablespoon drained capers
- ¼ teaspoon crushed red pepper flakes
- 1 pound (455 g) dried linguine
- 1 pound (455 g) large raw shrimp (31 to 35 per lb.), shelled and deveined

In a wide nonstick frying pan or wok, stir almonds over medium heat until golden beneath skins (about 8 minutes). Pour almonds into a food processor or blender; let cool. Then add parsley, ¼ cup (60 ml) of the oil, vinegar, garlic, capers, and red pepper flakes to processor. Whirl until pesto is smooth. Set aside.

In a 6- to 8-quart (6- to 8-liter) pan, cook linguine in about 4 quarts (3.8 liters) boiling water until just tender to bite (8 to 10 minutes); or cook according to package directions. Drain well, transfer to a warm wide bowl, and keep warm.

While pasta is cooking, heat remaining 1 teaspoon oil in frying pan or wok over medium-high heat. When oil is hot, add shrimp and stir-fry until just opaque in center; cut to test (3 to 4 minutes).

Spoon shrimp and pesto over pasta; mix gently but thoroughly. Makes 6 servings.

Per serving: 474 calories (29% calories from fat), 23 g protein, 61 g carbohydrates, 15 g total fat (2 g saturated fat), 93 mg cholesterol, 144 mg sodium

Soft Crab Tacos with Tomatillo-Lime Salsa

Pictured on facing page
Preparation time: About 20 minutes
Cooking time: About 15 minutes

•

Start with convenient cooked crabmeat to produce a speedy meal that's definitely out of the ordinary. Warm tortillas are topped with a blend of sweet crab, chiles, and tomatoes, then garnished with sour cream and tart tomatillo salsa. Use either corn or flour tortillas, as you prefer; you can warm them in the oven while you make the filling.

Tomatillo-Lime Salsa (recipe follows)

6 to 12 corn tortillas (*each* about 6 inches/15 cm in diameter) or low-fat flour tortillas (*each* 7 to 9 inches/18 to 23 cm in diameter)

2 tablespoons (30 ml) olive oil

1 clove garlic, minced or pressed

1 small red onion, finely chopped

1 can (about 4 oz./115 g) diced green chiles

2 large firm-ripe tomatoes (about 1 lb./455 g *total*), chopped

1 pound (455 g) cooked crabmeat

3 to 6 cups (3 to 6 oz./85 to 170 g) finely shredded lettuce

¼ cup (10 g) lightly packed cilantro leaves

Lime wedges

½ cup (120 ml) nonfat sour cream

Prepare Tomatillo-Lime Salsa; set aside. Brush tortillas lightly with hot water; then stack, wrap in foil, and heat in a 350°F/175°C oven until warm (10 to 12 minutes).

Meanwhile, heat oil in a wide nonstick frying pan or wok over medium-high heat. When oil is hot, add garlic and onion; stir-fry until onion begins to brown (about 5 minutes). Add chiles and half the tomatoes; stir-fry until tomatoes are soft (about 4 minutes). Remove from heat and gently stir in crab.

Divide lettuce equally among tortillas; then top tortillas equally with crab mixture, remaining tomatoes, and cilantro. Garnish with lime wedges; top with Tomatillo-Lime Salsa and sour cream. Makes 6 servings.

Tomatillo-Lime Salsa. In a medium-size bowl, combine 8 medium-size **tomatillos** (about 8 oz./230 g *total*), husked, rinsed, and finely chopped; 2 tablespoons sliced **green onion;** ¼ teaspoon **grated lime peel;** 2 tablespoons (30 ml) **lime juice;** 1 teaspoon **sugar** (or to taste); and about ⅛ teaspoon **salt** (or to taste). If made ahead, cover and refrigerate for up to 4 hours; stir before serving.

Per serving: 263 calories (25% calories from fat), 21 g protein, 29 g carbohydrates, 7 g total fat (0.9 g saturated fat), 76 mg cholesterol, 460 mg sodium

Stir-fried Cracked Crab with Onion

Preparation time: About 15 minutes
Cooking time: About 10 minutes

•

Some argue that cracked crab is best with no embellishments at all—but a taste of this dish might make such purists reconsider. It's simple to make: just heat the succulent crab pieces briefly in a simple, savory blend of sherry and oyster sauce.

⅓ cup (80 ml) *each* dry sherry and water

¼ cup (60 ml) oyster sauce or reduced-sodium soy sauce

2 teaspoons cornstarch

14 green onions

1 tablespoon (15 ml) salad oil

3 tablespoons minced fresh ginger

3 large cooked Dungeness crabs (about 6 lbs./2.7 kg *total*), cleaned and cracked

Continued on next page

A sophisticated but easy choice for light dining, these Soft Crab Tacos (recipe above) are filled with succulent shellfish and sprinkled with fresh tomato and cilantro. Top each serving with sour cream and tart Tomatillo-Lime Salsa.

Stir-fried Cracked Crab with Onion (continued)

In a small bowl, stir together sherry, water, oyster sauce, and cornstarch until blended; set aside. Trim and discard ends of onions; then cut onions into 2-inch (5-cm) lengths, keeping white and green parts separate.

Heat oil in a wide nonstick frying pan or wok over medium-high heat. Add ginger and white parts of onions; stir-fry until onions just begin to brown (about 2 minutes). Stir sherry mixture well and pour into pan; stir until sauce boils and thickens slightly (about 1 minute). Add crab and green parts of onions; stir to coat crab with sauce. Reduce heat to low, cover, and cook, stirring occasionally, until crab is heated through (5 to 8 minutes). Makes 6 servings.

Per serving: 163 calories (21% calories from fat), 21 g protein, 8 g carbohydrates, 3 g total fat (0.4 g saturated fat), 64 mg cholesterol, 805 mg sodium

Scallops with Broccoli & Bell Pepper

Preparation time: About 15 minutes
Cooking time: About 10 minutes

●

Simple, saucy, and bright—that describes this combination of green broccoli, red bell pepper, and white sea scallops. Serve the dish with fresh Chinese noodles or hot, fluffy rice.

Cooking Sauce (recipe follows)

1　pound (455 g) sea scallops

2　cups (145 g) broccoli flowerets

1　medium-size red or green bell pepper (about 6 oz./170 g), seeded and cut into thin strips

1　small onion, thinly sliced

2　teaspoons salad oil

1　or 2 cloves garlic, minced or pressed

Prepare Cooking Sauce and set aside.

Rinse scallops and pat dry; cut into bite-size pieces, if desired. Set aside.

In a wide nonstick frying pan or wok, combine broccoli, bell pepper, onion, and ⅓ cup (80 ml) water. Cover and cook over medium-high heat just until vegetables are

tender to bite (about 4 minutes). Uncover and stir-fry until liquid has evaporated. Stir Cooking Sauce well and pour into pan. Cook, stirring, until sauce boils and thickens slightly (1 to 2 minutes). Transfer vegetable mixture to a serving bowl and keep warm. Wipe pan clean (be careful; pan is hot).

Heat oil in pan over medium-high heat. When oil is hot, add garlic and 1 tablespoon (15 ml) water to pan. Stir-fry just until garlic is fragrant (about 30 seconds; do not scorch). Add scallops. Stir-fry until scallops are just opaque in center; cut to test (3 to 4 minutes). Pour scallops and any pan juices over vegetable mixture; mix gently but thoroughly. Makes 4 servings.

Cooking Sauce. In a small bowl, stir together 4 teaspoons **cornstarch** and 2 tablespoons (30 ml) **reduced-sodium soy sauce** until blended. Then stir in ¾ cup (180 ml) **fat-free reduced-sodium chicken broth**, 2 tablespoons (30 ml) **dry sherry**, 2 teaspoons finely minced **fresh ginger**, and 1½ teaspoons **sugar.**

Per serving: 196 calories (16% calories from fat), 23 g protein, 17 g carbohydrates, 3 g total fat (0.4 g saturated fat), 37 mg cholesterol, 591 mg sodium

Sautéed Scallops with Spinach & Farfalle

Preparation time: About 20 minutes
Cooking time: About 15 minutes

●

Whimsical pasta "butterflies" are a perfect foil for stir-fried scallops seasoned with sage. Add shredded spinach and diced tomato, and you have a hearty, fresh-tasting choice for lunch or a light supper.

8　ounces (230 g) dried farfalle or other pasta shapes (about 1½-inch/3.5-cm size)

1　pound (455 g) sea scallops

2　tablespoons (30 g) butter or margarine

2　cloves garlic, minced or pressed

　About ¾ teaspoon chopped fresh sage or ¼ teaspoon dried rubbed sage, or to taste

1　large tomato (about 8 oz./230 g), chopped and drained well

¼ cup (60 ml) dry white wine

½ to ¾ cup (15 to 23 g) finely shredded spinach

About ⅓ cup (30 g) grated Parmesan cheese

Sage sprigs

Pepper

In a 4- to 5-quart (3.8- to 5-liter) pan, cook farfalle in about 8 cups (1.9 liters) boiling water until just tender to bite (8 to 10 minutes); or cook according to package directions. Drain well, transfer to a warm rimmed platter, and keep warm.

While pasta is cooking, rinse scallops and pat dry; cut into bite-size pieces, if desired. Melt butter in a wide nonstick frying pan or wok over medium-high heat. Add scallops and stir-fry until just opaque in center; cut to test (3 to 4 minutes). Remove scallops from pan with a slotted spoon; keep warm.

Add garlic and chopped sage to pan; stir-fry just until garlic is fragrant (about 30 seconds; do not scorch). Stir in tomato and wine; bring to a boil. Remove from heat, add scallops and spinach, and mix gently but thoroughly. Spoon scallop mixture over pasta; sprinkle with cheese and garnish with sage sprigs. Season to taste with pepper. Makes 4 servings.

Per serving: 413 calories (21% calories from fat), 29 g protein, 48 g carbohydrates, 9 g total fat (5 g saturated fat), 58 mg cholesterol, 366 mg sodium

Red Snapper Stir-fry

Preparation time: About 20 minutes

Cooking time: About 10 minutes

Here's an interesting combination of sweet and savory flavors. Crunchy pea pods and chunks of mild snapper, cloaked in a sauce laced with ginger and garlic, are served over juicy fresh pineapple rings. On the side, offer a bulgur pilaf or steamed white or brown rice.

1 tablespoon finely minced fresh ginger

2 tablespoons (30 ml) *each* reduced-sodium soy sauce and unsweetened pineapple juice

2 cloves garlic, minced or pressed

1 teaspoon *each* sugar and Oriental sesame oil

⅛ teaspoon crushed red pepper flakes

1 pound (455 g) red snapper fillets (about ½ inch/1 cm thick), cut into 1-inch (2.5-cm) pieces

1 medium-size pineapple (3 to 3½ lbs./1.35 to 1.6 kg)

1 teaspoon salad oil

1½ cups (115 g) fresh Chinese pea pods (also called snow or sugar peas) or sugar snap peas, ends and strings removed; or 1 package (about 6 oz./170 g) frozen Chinese pea pods, thawed and drained

1 tablespoon cornstarch blended with 1 tablespoon (15 ml) cold water

½ cup (50 g) thinly sliced green onions

In a large bowl, stir together ginger, soy sauce, pineapple juice, garlic, sugar, sesame oil, and red pepper flakes. Add fish and stir to coat. Set aside; stir occasionally.

Peel and core pineapple, then cut crosswise into thin slices. Arrange slices on a rimmed platter; cover and set aside.

Heat salad oil in a wide nonstick frying pan or wok over medium-high heat. When oil is hot, add fish mixture and stir-fry gently until fish is just opaque but still moist in thickest part; cut to test (2 to 3 minutes). Remove fish from pan with a slotted spoon; keep warm.

Add pea pods to pan and stir-fry for 30 seconds (15 seconds if using frozen pea pods). Stir cornstarch mixture well, then pour into pan. Cook, stirring, until sauce boils and thickens slightly (1 to 2 minutes). Return fish to pan and add onions; mix gently but thoroughly, just until fish is hot and coated with sauce. Spoon fish mixture over pineapple slices. Makes 4 servings.

Per serving: 278 calories (15% calories from fat), 26 g protein, 34 g carbohydrates, 5 g total fat (0.7 g saturated fat), 42 mg cholesterol, 379 mg sodium

Salmon Sauté with Citrus Sauce

Pictured on facing page
Preparation time: About 30 minutes
Cooking time: About 10 minutes

•

A beautiful choice for a company meal, this stir-fry combines silky salmon with a trio of citrus fruits. Fresh orange, grapefruit, and lime segments, lightly warmed in a marmalade-sweetened sauce, mingle with the moist strips of fish. Complete the menu with steamed green beans and a loaf of crusty bread for soaking up the sauce.

3 or 4 medium-size oranges (1½ to 2 lbs. /680 to 905 g *total*)

1 large pink grapefruit (about 12 oz./340 g)

1 large lime (about 4 oz./115 g)

3 green onions

1 tablespoon butter or margarine

1 pound (455 g) salmon fillets (about ½ inch/1 cm thick), skinned and cut into 1- by 2-inch (2.5- by 5-cm) strips

¼ cup (60 ml) dry vermouth

⅓ cup (100 g) orange marmalade

1 tablespoon chopped fresh mint

  Mint sprigs (optional)

  Salt and pepper

Shred enough peel (colored part only) from oranges, grapefruit, and lime to make ½ teaspoon of each kind of peel. Combine peels in a small bowl; cover and set aside.

Cut off and discard remaining peel and all white membrane from grapefruit, lime, and 2 of the oranges. Holding fruit over a bowl to catch juice, cut between membranes to release segments; set segments aside. Pour juice from bowl into a glass measure. Squeeze juice from remaining oranges; add enough of this orange juice to juice in glass measure to make ½ cup/120 ml (reserve remaining orange juice for other uses). Set juice aside.

Trim and discard ends of onions. Cut onions into 2-inch (5-cm) lengths, then cut each piece lengthwise into slivers; set aside.

Melt butter in a wide nonstick frying pan or wok over medium-high heat. Add fish. Stir-fry gently (flipping with

a spatula, if needed) until fish is just opaque but still moist in thickest part; cut to test (about 4 minutes). With a slotted spoon, transfer fish to a large bowl; keep warm.

Add citrus juices and vermouth to pan. Bring to a boil; then boil, stirring often, until reduced to ⅓ cup/80 ml (about 3 minutes). Reduce heat to low, add marmalade, and stir until melted. Add onions and citrus segments; stir gently just until heated through. Remove from heat and stir in chopped mint.

Spoon fruit sauce over fish; mix gently. Divide fish mixture among 4 individual rimmed plates; garnish with citrus peels and mint sprigs, if desired. Season to taste with salt and pepper. Makes 4 servings.

Per serving: 351 calories (27% calories from fat), 24 g protein, 39 g carbohydrates, 10 g total fat (3 g saturated fat), 70 mg cholesterol, 98 mg sodium

Stir-fried Salmon with Creamy Tomatillo Sauce

Preparation time: About 20 minutes
Cooking time: About 15 minutes

•

Rich pink salmon served on a creamy, pale green tomatillo sauce makes a lovely entrée. Before using fresh tomatillos, remove the husks and rinse the fruit well to remove its sticky coating.

4 medium-size tomatillos (about 4 oz./115 g *total*), husked, rinsed, and chopped

1 tablespoon sliced green onion

1 clove garlic, peeled

¼ teaspoon grated lime peel

1 tablespoon (15 ml) lime juice

  About ¾ teaspoon sugar, or to taste

⅛ teaspoon salt

Continued on page 60

· ·

Brilliant orange, grapefruit, and lime all come together in Salmon Sauté with Citrus Sauce (recipe at left). Lean and lovely to look at, it's just right for a special occasion.

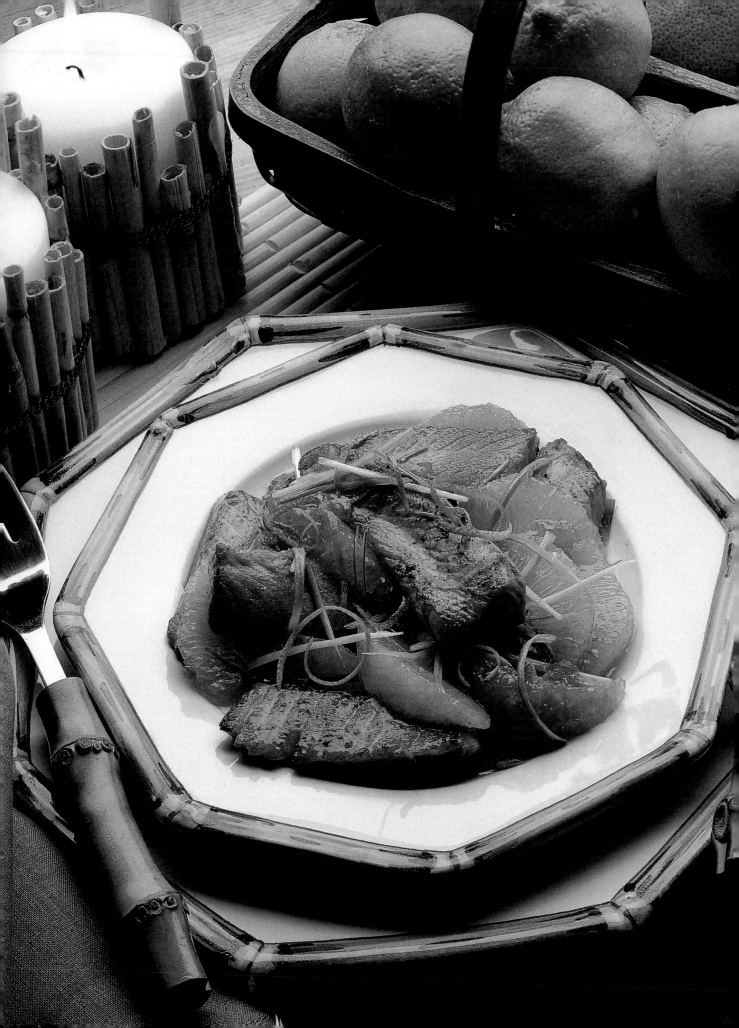

Stir-fried Salmon with Creamy Tomatillo Sauce (continued)

- ½ cup (120 ml) plain low-fat yogurt (do not use nonfat yogurt) blended with 2 teaspoons cornstarch
- 8 low-fat flour tortillas (*each* 7 to 9 inches/18 to 23 cm in diameter)
- 1 tablespoon butter or margarine
- 1 pound (455 g) salmon fillets (about ½ inch/1 cm thick), skinned and cut into ¾-inch (2-cm) pieces
- 1 medium-size tomato (about 6 oz./170 g), chopped and drained well
- 2 tablespoons cilantro leaves

  Lime wedges

  Ground white pepper

In a blender or food processor, combine tomatillos, onion, garlic, lime peel, lime juice, sugar, and salt. Whirl until smooth. By hand, stir in yogurt mixture just until combined; do not overbeat or sauce will separate. Set aside.

Brush tortillas lightly with hot water; then stack, wrap in foil, and heat in a 350°F/175°C oven until warm (10 to 12 minutes).

Meanwhile, melt butter in a wide nonstick frying pan or wok over medium-high heat. Add fish and stir-fry gently until just opaque but still moist in thickest part; cut to test (about 4 minutes). Remove from pan and keep warm. Wipe pan clean (be careful; pan is hot).

Add yogurt-tomatillo sauce to pan. Reduce heat to medium-low and simmer gently, stirring constantly, until sauce is slightly thickened (2 to 3 minutes); do not boil.

Divide sauce among 4 individual rimmed plates; spread sauce out evenly, then top equally with fish. Sprinkle with tomato and cilantro leaves, garnish with lime wedges, and season to taste with white pepper. Serve with tortillas. Makes 4 servings.

Per serving: 370 calories (27% calories from fat), 29 g protein, 44 g carbohydrates, 12 g total fat (3 g saturated fat), 72 mg cholesterol, 533 mg sodium

Sea Bass with Green Beans & Sesame-Orange Sauce

Preparation time: About 20 minutes
Cooking time: About 15 minutes

•

Mild, rich-tasting Chilean sea bass, red onion, and slender green beans combine in this simple dish. Sea bass is often sold in 1-inch-thick (2.5-cm-thick) fillets; if necessary, cut the pieces horizontally to make them ½ inch (1 cm) thick.

  Sesame-Orange Sauce (recipe follows)
- 1 teaspoon sesame seeds
- 8 ounces (230 g) slender green beans (ends removed), cut diagonally into 1-inch (2.5-cm) lengths
- ½ cup (60 g) sliced red onion
- 1 teaspoon salad oil or olive oil
- 1 pound (455 g) Chilean sea bass, halibut, or orange roughy fillets (about ½ inch/1 cm thick), cut into 1-inch (2.5-cm) pieces

Prepare Sesame-Orange Sauce and set aside.

In a wide nonstick frying pan or wok, stir sesame seeds over medium heat until golden (about 3 minutes). Pour out of pan and set aside.

In pan, combine beans, onion, and ⅓ cup (80 ml) water. Increase heat to medium-high; cover and cook until beans are almost tender to bite (about 3 minutes). Uncover and stir-fry until liquid has evaporated. Transfer bean mixture to a rimmed platter and keep warm.

Heat oil in pan. When oil is hot, add fish and stir-fry gently until just opaque but still moist in thickest part; cut to test (3 to 4 minutes). Remove fish from pan with a slotted spoon; add to bean mixture and mix gently but thoroughly. Sprinkle with sesame seeds. Stir Sesame-Orange Sauce; offer sauce to add to individual servings. Makes 4 servings.

Sesame-Orange Sauce. In a small bowl, stir together ¾ teaspoon **grated orange peel**, ¼ cup (60 ml) **orange juice**, 2 tablespoons (30 ml) **reduced-sodium soy sauce,**

1 clove **garlic** (minced or pressed), 1½ teaspoons **honey,** 1 teaspoon minced **fresh ginger,** and ½ teaspoon **Oriental sesame oil.**

Per serving: 178 calories (23% calories from fat), 23 g protein, 11 g carbohydrates, 4 g total fat (0.9 g saturated fat), 46 mg cholesterol, 383 mg sodium

Stir-fried Tuna on Spinach

Preparation time: About 30 minutes
Cooking time: About 8 minutes

•

Here's an eye-catching entrée: hot, gingery fresh tuna over cool, crisp spinach leaves.

> **Soy Dressing (recipe follows)**
> 3 **quarts (about 12 oz./340 g) lightly packed rinsed, crisped spinach leaves**
> 1 **tablespoon sesame seeds**
> 1 **teaspoon salad oil**
> 2 **tablespoons finely minced fresh ginger**
> 12 **ounces (340 g) fresh tuna, cut into ½- by 2-inch (1- by 5-cm) strips**
> ½ **cup (50 g) thinly sliced green onions**
> 1 **cup (115 g) thinly sliced red radishes**
> **Whole green onions (ends trimmed)**

Prepare Soy Dressing; set aside. Arrange spinach on a large platter, cover, and set aside.

In a wide nonstick frying pan or wok, stir sesame seeds over medium heat until golden (about 3 minutes). Pour out of pan and set aside.

Heat oil in pan over medium-high heat. When oil is hot, add ginger and stir-fry just until lightly browned (about 30 seconds; do not scorch). Add tuna and stir-fry gently (flipping with a spatula, if needed) until just opaque but still moist and pink in thickest part; cut to test (about 3 minutes). Stir Soy Dressing and pour into pan; stir to mix, then remove pan from heat.

Spoon tuna mixture over spinach on platter. Sprinkle with sliced onions, radishes, and sesame seeds. Garnish with whole onions. Makes 4 servings.

Soy Dressing. In a small bowl, stir together ¼ cup (60

ml) **mirin** or cream sherry, 6 tablespoons (85 ml) **unseasoned rice vinegar** or cider vinegar, 2 tablespoons (30 ml) **reduced-sodium soy sauce,** and 1 teaspoon **prepared horseradish.**

Per serving: 223 calories (30% calories from fat), 24 g protein, 13 g carbohydrates, 7 g total fat (1 g saturated fat), 32 mg cholesterol, 415 mg sodium

Swordfish with Mango Relish

Preparation time: About 10 minutes, plus 30 minutes to soak onion
Cooking time: About 5 minutes

•

The bright colors and bold flavors of this savory-sweet fruit relish really bounce out at you! Serve it over thin strips of swordfish, quickly stir-fried to stay succulent.

> **Mango Relish (recipe follows)**
> 2 **teaspoons salad oil**
> 1½ **pounds (680 g) swordfish, cut into ½- by 2-inch (1- by 5-cm) strips**
> ½ **cup (20 g) lightly packed cilantro sprigs**

Prepare Mango Relish and set aside.

Heat oil in a wide nonstick frying pan or wok over medium-high heat. When oil is hot, add swordfish and stir-fry gently (flipping with a spatula, if needed) until just opaque but still moist in thickest part; cut to test (about 4 minutes). Spoon swordfish onto a platter; top with Mango Relish and garnish with cilantro sprigs. Makes 6 servings.

Mango Relish. Place ¼ cup (45 g) minced **white onion** in a fine strainer; rinse with cold water. Then place onion in a bowl, cover with **ice water,** and let stand for 30 minutes. Drain. Return onion to bowl; stir in 1½ cups (250 g) diced **ripe mango,** ¾ cup (115 g) diced **red bell pepper,** ¼ cup (10 g) chopped **cilantro,** 1 tablespoon minced **fresh ginger,** and 2 tablespoons (30 ml) **lemon juice.**

Per serving: 186 calories (30% calories from fat), 23 g protein, 9 g carbohydrates, 6 g total fat (1 g saturated fat), 44 mg cholesterol, 106 mg sodium

Meat Dishes

*L*amb curry, veal piccata, sweet and sour pork, Jamaican-style jerk beef—yes, you'll find them all on our low-fat menus! What's more, we've adapted these and other flavor-rich favorites for stir-frying, so you can cook them quickly.

....

Garnished with fresh mint, aromatic Curried Lamb (recipe on page 64) is served on a platter of fluffy couscous. Offer fresh Grape Chutney (recipe on page 52) alongside the juicy chunks of lamb and tender-crisp tiny onions.

Curried Lamb with Grape Chutney

Pictured on page 62
Preparation time: About 25 minutes
Cooking time: About 45 minutes

●

To add interest to a simple lamb curry, serve it with warm homemade grape-apple chutney; while the chutney simmers, you can easily cook the meat and a pan of fluffy couscous. If you prefer, make the chutney in advance to serve cold.

> Grape Chutney (page 52)
>
> 1 pound (455 g) lean boneless leg of lamb, trimmed of fat and cut into 1-inch (2.5-cm) cubes
>
> 10 ounces (285 g) tiny onions (*each* about ¾ inch/2 cm in diameter), peeled
>
> 2½ teaspoons curry powder
>
> ¼ teaspoon salt
>
> 1½ cups (360 ml) fat-free reduced-sodium chicken broth
>
> 1 cup (185 g) couscous
>
> 1 tablespoon (15 ml) olive oil
>
> 1 tablespoon chopped fresh mint, or to taste
>
> Mint sprigs

Prepare Grape Chutney. When chutney is almost done, combine lamb, onions, curry powder, and salt in a large bowl; turn meat and onions to coat with seasonings. Set aside.

In a 3- to 4-quart (2.8- to 3.8-liter) pan, bring broth to a boil over high heat; stir in couscous. Cover, remove from heat, and let stand until liquid has been absorbed (about 5 minutes). Keep warm; fluff occasionally with a fork.

While couscous is standing, heat oil in a wide nonstick frying pan or wok over medium-high heat. When oil is hot, add lamb and onions. Stir-fry just until onions are heated through and meat is done to your liking; cut to test (5 to 7 minutes for medium-rare). Add water, 1 tablespoon (15 ml) at a time, if pan appears dry.

Spoon couscous onto a rimmed platter. Spoon meat and onions over couscous; sprinkle with chopped mint. Garnish with mint sprigs. Offer Grape Chutney to add to taste. Makes 4 servings.

Per serving: 549 calories (18% calories from fat), 33 g protein, 80 g carbohydrates, 11 g total fat (3 g saturated fat), 75 mg cholesterol, 336 mg sodium

Hunan Lamb

Preparation time: About 25 minutes, plus at least 1 hour to soak Green Onion Brushes (if used)
Cooking time: About 25 minutes

●

To temper the heat of this spicy lamb, offer rice and a crisp, cooling salad of greens, cucumbers, and fresh orange segments. Frilly green onion "brushes" make a pretty garnish; if you want to use them, be sure to allow an extra hour to soak the onion pieces in ice water.

> Green Onion Brushes (optional; page 85)
>
> 1 cup (185 g) long-grain white rice
>
> 1 tablespoon cornstarch
>
> 2 tablespoons (30 ml) reduced-sodium soy sauce
>
> 1 large egg white
>
> 2 tablespoons (30 ml) lemon juice
>
> 1 teaspoon honey
>
> 1 pound (455 g) lean boneless leg of lamb, trimmed of fat and cut into ⅛- by 2-inch (3-mm by 5-cm) strips
>
> Cooking Sauce (recipe follows)
>
> 3 green onions
>
> 1 teaspoon salad oil
>
> 2 cloves garlic, minced or pressed
>
> Hot Chili Oil (page 69) or purchased hot chili oil (optional)

Prepare Green Onion Brushes, if desired. Set aside.

In a 3- to 4-quart (2.8- to 3.8-liter) pan, bring 2 cups (470 ml) water to a boil over high heat; stir in rice. Reduce heat, cover, and simmer until liquid has been absorbed and rice is tender to bite (about 20 minutes).

Meanwhile, in a large bowl, stir together cornstarch and soy sauce until blended. Add egg white, lemon juice, and honey; beat until blended. Add lamb and stir to coat. Set aside; stir occasionally.

Prepare Cooking Sauce and set aside. Trim and discard ends of whole green onions; cut onions into 2-inch lengths, then sliver each piece lengthwise and set aside.

Heat salad oil in a wide nonstick frying pan or wok over medium-high heat. When oil is hot, add garlic and stir-fry just until fragrant (about 30 seconds; do not scorch). Lift meat from marinade and drain well (discard marinade). Add meat to pan and stir-fry until done to your liking; cut to test (1 to 2 minutes for medium-rare). Stir Cooking Sauce well and pour into pan. Cook, stirring, until sauce boils and thickens slightly (1 to 2 minutes). Remove from heat and stir in slivered onions.

Spoon rice onto a rimmed platter; spoon meat mixture over rice. Garnish with Green Onion Brushes, if desired. Offer chili oil to add to taste, if desired. Makes 4 servings.

Cooking Sauce. In a small bowl, stir together 3 tablespoons (45 ml) **hoisin sauce,** 2 tablespoons (30 ml) **seasoned rice vinegar** (or 2 tablespoons/30 ml distilled white vinegar plus ¾ teaspoon sugar), 2 tablespoons **chili paste with garlic,** 2 to 3 teaspoons **sugar,** and 2 teaspoons **Oriental sesame oil.**

Per serving: 457 calories (25% calories from fat), 28 g protein, 55 g carbohydrates, 12 g total fat (3 g saturated fat), 73 mg cholesterol, 807 mg sodium

Sautéed Lamb with Apples

Preparation time: About 20 minutes
Cooking time: About 10 minutes

•

Sliced, stir-fried Golden Delicious apples, sauced with a tart-sweet blend of apple jelly and cider vinegar, make a great partner for tender lamb. For an attractive presentation, serve the meat in red-violet radicchio cups.

4 to 8 large radicchio leaves, rinsed and crisped

1 pound (455 g) lean boneless leg of lamb, trimmed of fat and cut into ¾-inch (2-cm) chunks

¼ teaspoon salt

⅛ teaspoon pepper

⅓ cup (80 ml) apple jelly

⅓ cup (80 ml) cider vinegar

1 tablespoon cornstarch blended with 1 tablespoon (15 ml) cold water

1 teaspoon Dijon mustard

¾ teaspoon chopped fresh thyme or ¼ teaspoon dried thyme

⅓ cup (50 g) dried currants or raisins

3 large Golden Delicious apples (about 1½ lbs./680 g *total*), peeled, cored, and sliced ¼ to ½ inch (6 mm to 1 cm) thick

2 teaspoons salad oil

1 to 2 tablespoons chopped parsley

Thyme sprigs

Arrange 1 or 2 radicchio leaves (overlapping, if necessary) on each of 4 individual plates; cover and set aside.

In a large bowl, mix lamb, salt, and pepper; set aside. In a small bowl, stir together jelly, 3 tablespoons (45 ml) of the vinegar, cornstarch mixture, mustard, and chopped thyme until well blended. Stir in currants and set aside. In a medium-size bowl, gently mix apples with remaining vinegar.

Heat 1 teaspoon of the oil in a wide nonstick frying pan or wok over medium-high heat. When oil is hot, add apples and stir-fry gently until almost tender when pierced (about 4 minutes). Add water, 1 tablespoon (15 ml) at a time, if pan appears dry. Stir jelly mixture well; pour into pan and cook, stirring, just until sauce boils and thickens slightly (1 to 2 minutes). Remove apple mixture from pan and keep warm. Wipe pan clean (be careful; pan is hot).

Heat remaining 1 teaspoon oil in pan over medium-high heat. When oil is hot, add meat and stir-fry just until done to your liking; cut to test (about 3 minutes for medium-rare). Remove from heat and stir in parsley.

Spoon meat equally into radicchio leaves; spoon apple mixture alongside. Garnish with thyme sprigs. Makes 4 servings.

Per serving: 367 calories (19% calories from fat), 25 g protein, 52 g carbohydrates, 8 g total fat (2 g saturated fat), 73 mg cholesterol, 114 mg sodium

Garlic Beef in Pita Bread

Pictured on facing page
Preparation time: About 15 minutes
Cooking time: About 15 minutes

•

Stir-fries make great hot fillings for pita breads. These sandwiches are stuffed with mixed greens and garlicky strips of sirloin; a minted yogurt sauce adds a cool, refreshing accent.

Cool Yogurt Sauce (page 52)

4 to 6 cloves garlic, minced or pressed

3 tablespoons (45 ml) reduced-sodium soy sauce

1½ teaspoons sugar

⅛ teaspoon crushed red pepper flakes

1 pound (455 g) lean boneless top sirloin steak (about 1 inch/2.5 cm thick), trimmed of fat and cut across the grain into ⅛- by 2-inch (3-mm by 5-cm) strips

3 green onions

1 teaspoon salad oil

1 teaspoon cornstarch blended with 1 teaspoon cold water

5 to 6 cups (5 to 6 oz./140 to 170 g) mixed salad greens, rinsed and crisped

4 pita breads (*each* about 6 inches/15 cm in diameter), cut crosswise into halves

Prepare Cool Yogurt Sauce and set aside.

In a large bowl, stir together garlic, soy sauce, sugar, and red pepper flakes. Add steak and stir to coat. Set aside; stir occasionally. Trim and discard ends of onions; then cut onions into 1-inch (2.5-cm) lengths and sliver each piece lengthwise. Set aside.

Heat oil in a wide nonstick frying pan or wok over medium-high heat. When oil is hot, lift meat from marinade and drain briefly (reserve marinade). Add meat to pan and stir-fry until done to your liking; cut to test (2 to 3 minutes for rare). With a slotted spoon, transfer meat to a bowl; keep warm.

Stir cornstarch mixture well; pour into pan along with reserved marinade and any meat juices that have accumulated in bowl. Cook, stirring, until sauce boils and thickens slightly (1 to 2 minutes). Remove pan from heat and stir in meat and onions.

To serve, divide salad greens equally among pita bread halves; then spoon in meat mixture. Drizzle Cool Yogurt Sauce over meat. Makes 4 servings.

Per serving: 386 calories (17% calories from fat), 34 g protein, 44 g carbohydrates, 7 g total fat (2 g saturated fat), 70 mg cholesterol, 886 mg sodium

Stir-fried Beef & Asparagus

Preparation time: About 15 minutes
Cooking time: About 10 minutes

•

This elegant-looking dish gets its wonderful sunny, fruity flavor from orange juice and raspberries.

½ cup (120 ml) dry red wine

¼ cup (60 ml) orange juice

2 tablespoons (30 ml) raspberry or red wine vinegar

¼ cup (40 g) finely chopped shallots

2 teaspoons chopped fresh tarragon or ½ teaspoon dried tarragon

1 pound (455 g) lean boneless top sirloin steak (about 1 inch/2.5 cm thick), trimmed of fat and cut across the grain into ⅛- by 2-inch (3-mm by 5-cm) strips

1½ pounds (680 g) asparagus

1 teaspoon olive oil

About ½ cup (60 g) fresh raspberries

In a large bowl, stir together wine, orange juice, vinegar, shallots, and tarragon. Add steak and stir to coat. Set aside; stir occasionally.

Snap off and discard tough ends of asparagus; then
Continued on page 71

....

For a casual and satisfying dinner, accompany zesty Garlic Beef in Pita Bread (recipe at left) with refreshing Cool Yogurt Sauce (recipe on page 52) and your favorite red wine.

Flavored Oils

Infused with the essence of spices or herbs, flavored oils add excitement to any stir-fry. You can use a teaspoon or two in place of some of the salad or olive oil used for cooking; or, at the table, offer a cruet of oil to sprinkle over your favorite meat or vegetable combinations.

On these pages, we tell you how to make six flavored oils: curry, basil, ginger, garlic, hot chili, and thyme. As the base, use salad oil, virgin olive oil, or light olive oil. Avoid extra-virgin olive oil—it's so strong that it may overwhelm the flavors of the ingredients added to it. Heat the oil and flavoring just until warm; if the mixture gets too hot, the spices may scorch or burn.

Once the oil has been infused, simply pour it from the pan, leaving the herb or spice residue behind. Or, if you like, strain the oil. To do this, line a fine strainer with a single layer of muslin or a double layer of cheesecloth and set it over a clean, dry, deep bowl. Pour the oil mixture through; press the residue with the back of a clean, dry spoon to extract as much oil as possible, then discard the residue.

Store flavored oils in clean, dry glass bottles or jars. If you see sediment upon standing, pour off (or strain) the oil again, leaving the sediment behind. These oils keep well at room temperature, but you can refrigerate them if you prefer. Chilled olive oil will turn cloudy and thick, but will become clear and pourable again when returned to room temperature.

Note: Like any other oil, these flavored oils get almost all their calories from fat. Nonetheless, if used sparingly, they still have a place in a low-fat diet.

Curry Oil

Preparation time: About 5 minutes
Cooking time: About 5 minutes

•

¼ cup (15 g) curry powder
1 cup (240 ml) salad oil or olive oil
1 to 3 cinnamon sticks (*each about 3 inches/8 cm long*)

In a small pan, whisk together curry powder and ¼ cup (60 ml) of the oil until well blended. Gradually whisk in remaining ¾ cup (180 ml) oil. Add cinnamon stick(s). Heat over medium heat, stirring often, just until warm (*not* hot or boiling). Remove from heat and let cool slightly.

With a clean, dry slotted spoon, lift out cinnamon stick(s); set aside.

Carefully pour oil into a clean, dry glass bottle or jar, leaving curry sediment behind; discard sediment. (Or strain oil, if desired.) Add cinnamon stick(s) to bottle; cover airtight and store for up to 6 months. Makes about 1 cup (240 ml).

Basil Oil

Preparation time: About 10 minutes
Cooking time: About 10 minutes

•

½ cup (20 g) firmly packed fresh basil leaves
1 cup (240 ml) salad oil or olive oil

In a 4- to 5-quart (3.8- to 5-liter) pan, bring 8 cups (1.9 liters) water to a boil over high heat. Drop basil into boiling water and cook just until bright green (about 3 seconds); immediately drain, then plunge into ice water until cool. Drain basil well again; blot dry.

In a blender or food processor, combine basil and ¼ cup (60 ml) of the oil. Whirl until well blended. Add remaining ¾ cup (180 ml) oil and whirl until smoothly puréed. Transfer oil mixture to a small pan and heat over medium heat, stirring occasionally, just until warm (*not* hot or boiling). Remove from heat and let cool slightly.

Carefully pour oil into a clean, dry glass bottle or jar, leaving basil sediment behind; discard sediment. (Or strain oil, if desired.) Cover airtight and store for up to 6 months. Makes about 1 cup (240 ml).

Ginger Oil

Preparation time: About 5 minutes
Cooking time: About 5 minutes

•

¼ cup (15 g) ground ginger
1 cup (240 ml) salad oil or olive oil

In a small pan, whisk together ginger and ¼ cup (60 ml) of the oil until well blended. Gradually whisk in remaining ¾ cup (180 ml) oil. Heat over medium heat, stirring often, just until warm (*not* hot or boiling). Remove from heat and let cool slightly.

Carefully pour oil into a clean, dry glass bottle or jar, leaving ginger sediment behind; discard sediment. (Or strain oil, if desired.) Cover airtight and store for up to 6 months. Makes about 1 cup (240 ml).

Garlic Oil

Preparation time: About 10 minutes
Cooking time: About 15 minutes

•

1 medium-size head garlic (about 3 oz./85 g)
About 1 cup (240 ml) salad oil or olive oil

Separate garlic into cloves; then peel and thinly slice garlic cloves. Heat ⅓ cup (80 ml) of the oil in a wide

nonstick frying pan or wok over medium-low heat. Add garlic and stir-fry until tinged with gold (about 10 minutes; do not scorch). If pan appears dry or garlic sticks to pan, add more oil, 1 tablespoon (15 ml) at a time.

Add ⅔ cup (160 ml) more oil to pan. Increase heat to medium and stir often just until oil is warm (*not* hot or boiling). Remove from heat and let cool slightly.

With a clean, dry slotted spoon, lift garlic from pan; discard garlic (garlic left in oil may spoil). Then carefully pour oil into a clean, dry glass bottle or jar. (Or strain oil, if desired.) Cover airtight and store for up to 6 months. Makes about 1 cup (240 ml).

Hot Chili Oil

Preparation time: About 5 minutes
Cooking time: About 5 minutes

•

6 to 12 small dried hot red chiles (use the greater number of chiles for more heat)

1 cup (240 ml) salad oil or olive oil

Place 3 whole chiles in a small pan; add oil. Split each of the remaining 3 to 9 chiles in half; add to pan. Heat over medium heat, stirring gently, just until warm (*not* hot or boiling). Remove from heat and let cool slightly.

With a clean, dry slotted spoon, remove split chiles and seeds from oil; discard. Remove whole chiles; set aside. Carefully pour oil into a clean, dry glass bottle or jar. (Or strain oil, if desired.) Add whole chiles to bottle; cover airtight and store for up to 6 months. Makes about 1 cup (240 ml).

Thyme Oil

Preparation time: About 5 minutes
Cooking time: About 5 minutes

•

¼ cup (10 g) chopped fresh thyme
1 cup (240 ml) salad oil or olive oil

In a small pan, whisk together thyme and ¼ cup (60 ml) of the oil until well blended. Gradually whisk in remaining ¾ cup (180 ml) oil. Heat over medium heat, stirring often, just until warm (*not* hot or boiling). Remove from heat and let cool slightly.

Carefully pour oil into a clean, dry glass bottle or jar, leaving thyme sediment behind; discard sediment. (Or strain oil, if desired.) Cover airtight and store for up to 6 months. Makes about 1 cup (240 ml).

Stir-fried Beef & Asparagus (continued)

cut spears into 3-inch (8-cm) lengths. Place asparagus and ½ cup (120 ml) water in a wide nonstick frying pan or wok. Cover; cook over medium-high heat, stirring occasionally, until asparagus is tender-crisp to bite (4 to 5 minutes). Drain asparagus, transfer to a platter, and keep warm. Wipe pan dry (be careful; pan is hot).

Heat oil in pan over medium-high heat. When oil is hot, lift meat from marinade and drain briefly; reserve ¼ cup (60 ml) of the marinade. Add meat to pan and stir-fry until done to your liking; cut to test (2 to 3 minutes for rare). Add the reserved ¼ cup (60 ml) marinade and bring to a boil. Spoon meat mixture over asparagus; top with raspberries. Makes 4 servings.

Per serving: 213 calories (29% calories from fat), 27 g protein, 8 g carbohydrates, 6 g total fat (2 g saturated fat), 69 mg cholesterol, 70 mg sodium

Veal with Apricot Salsa

Pictured on facing page
Preparation time: About 25 minutes
Cooking time: About 25 minutes

•

A nontraditional warm salsa of fresh tomatoes, sautéed onion, and dried apricots soaked in lime juice makes this dish unusual. Be sure not to overcook the veal—after only a minute or two of stir-frying, it will be done just right.

- 1 cup (185 g) long-grain white rice
- ⅔ cup (90 g) chopped dried apricots
- ¼ cup (60 ml) lime juice
- ¾ cup (240 g) apricot jam or preserves
- 1 tablespoon firmly packed brown sugar
- ½ teaspoon ground cinnamon
- ¼ teaspoon *each* salt and liquid hot pepper seasoning
- 1 small onion, chopped

- 2 large tomatoes (about 1 lb./455 g *total*), chopped and drained well
- 1 teaspoon olive oil or salad oil
- 1 pound (455 g) veal scaloppine, cut into ¼- by 2-inch (6-mm by 5-cm) strips
- 2 cloves garlic, minced or pressed
- 3 tablespoons chopped cilantro
   Cilantro sprigs

In a 3- to 4-quart (2.8- to 3.8-liter) pan, bring 2 cups (470 ml) water to a boil over high heat; stir in rice. Reduce heat, cover, and simmer until liquid has been absorbed and rice is tender to bite (about 20 minutes).

Meanwhile, in a small bowl, combine apricots and lime juice; let stand until apricots are softened (about 10 minutes), stirring occasionally. In another small bowl, stir together jam, ¼ cup (60 ml) water, sugar, cinnamon, salt, and hot pepper seasoning.

In a wide nonstick frying pan or wok, combine onion and 2 tablespoons (30 ml) water. Stir-fry over medium-high heat until onion is soft (about 4 minutes). Add more water, 1 tablespoon (15 ml) at a time, if pan appears dry. Add apricot–lime juice mixture and jam mixture. Cook, stirring, until almost all liquid has evaporated (about 5 minutes). Transfer to a large bowl and add tomatoes; mix gently. Wipe pan clean (be careful; pan is hot).

Heat oil in pan over medium-high heat. When oil is hot, add veal, 1 tablespoon (15 ml) water, and garlic. Stir-fry just until meat is no longer pink on outside (1 to 2 minutes). Remove meat from pan with a slotted spoon; add to apricot-tomato salsa. Then add chopped cilantro; mix gently but thoroughly.

Spoon rice into individual bowls and top with meat mixture. Garnish with cilantro sprigs. Makes 4 servings.

Per serving: 551 calories (6% calories from fat), 30 g protein, 102 g carbohydrates, 4 g total fat (0.9 g saturated fat), 89 mg cholesterol, 260 mg sodium

···

A tangy salsa of dried fruit and fresh vegetables gives this impressive main dish its irresistible flavor. Spoon Veal with Apricot Salsa (recipe above) over hot cooked rice and garnish with sprigs of fresh cilantro.

Veal with Mushrooms

Preparation time: About 20 minutes
Cooking time: About 15 minutes

•

Marsala flavors a mild stir-fry of veal and sliced mushrooms to spoon over hot linguine.

- 1 **pound (455 g) veal scaloppine, cut into ¼- by 2-inch (6-mm by 5-cm) strips**
- ⅛ **teaspoon** *each* **salt and pepper**
- 8 **ounces (230 g) dried linguine**
- 1 **tablespoon butter or margarine**
- 2 **cloves garlic, minced or pressed**
- 2 **cups (170 g) sliced mushrooms**
- ½ **cup (120 ml) marsala or cream sherry**
- 3 **tablespoons chopped parsley**
- 1 **large tomato (about 8 oz./230 g), chopped and drained well**
- ¼ **cup (35 g) pitted ripe olives, chopped**

In a large bowl, mix veal, salt, and pepper; set aside.

In a 4- to 5-quart (3.8- to 5-liter) pan, cook linguine in about 8 cups (1.9 liters) boiling water until just tender to bite (8 to 10 minutes); or cook according to package directions. Drain well, transfer to a warm rimmed platter, and keep warm.

While pasta is cooking, melt butter in a wide nonstick frying pan or wok over medium-high heat. Add meat and garlic; stir-fry just until meat is no longer pink on outside (1 to 2 minutes). Add water, 1 tablespoon (15 ml) at a time, if pan appears dry. Remove meat from pan with a slotted spoon; keep warm.

Add mushrooms and 3 tablespoons (45 ml) water to pan. Stir-fry until mushrooms are soft (about 3 minutes), gently scraping any browned bits free from pan. Add marsala and bring to a boil; then boil, stirring, until sauce is slightly thickened (about 3 minutes). Remove pan from heat and stir in meat and parsley.

Spoon meat mixture over pasta; sprinkle with tomato and olives. Makes 4 servings.

Per serving: 440 calories (16% calories from fat), 33 g protein, 52 g carbohydrates, 7 g total fat (3 g saturated fat), 96 mg cholesterol, 191 mg sodium

Stir-fried Veal Piccata

Preparation time: About 15 minutes
Cooking time: About 10 minutes

•

Thin, tender strips of veal and a piquant lemon-caper sauce give this lean stir-fry the flavor of a classic veal piccata. You might serve it with steamed asparagus and a basket of crisp-crusted French rolls.

Cooking Sauce (recipe follows)
- 1 **pound (455 g) veal scaloppine, cut into ¼- by 2-inch (6-mm by 5-cm) strips**
- ½ **teaspoon paprika**
- ¼ **teaspoon grated lemon peel**
- ⅛ **teaspoon salt**
- 1 **teaspoon butter or margarine**
- 1 **teaspoon olive oil**
- ½ **teaspoon cornstarch blended with 1 teaspoon cold water**
- 2 **tablespoons drained capers, or to taste**
  Chopped parsley and lemon wedges
  Pepper

Prepare Cooking Sauce; set aside.

In a large bowl, combine veal, paprika, lemon peel, and salt. Melt butter in oil in a wide nonstick frying pan or wok over medium-high heat. When butter mixture is hot, add meat mixture; stir-fry just until meat is no longer pink on outside (1 to 2 minutes). With a slotted spoon, transfer meat to a rimmed platter; keep warm.

Stir Cooking Sauce well; pour into pan. Bring to a boil; then boil, stirring, for 3 minutes. Stir cornstarch mixture well; add to pan along with capers. Cook, stirring, until sauce boils and thickens slightly (about 1 minute). Spoon sauce over meat; garnish with parsley and lemon wedges. Season to taste with pepper. Makes 4 servings.

Cooking Sauce. In a small bowl, stir together ½ cup (120 ml) **dry white wine,** 2 tablespoons (30 ml) **lemon juice,** and 1½ teaspoons **honey.**

Per serving: 172 calories (25% calories from fat), 24 g protein, 3 g carbohydrates, 4 g total fat (1 g saturated fat), 91 mg cholesterol, 265 mg sodium

Chile Beef Burritos

Preparation time: About 15 minutes
Cooking time: About 15 minutes

•

Don't let the cayenne-and-jalapeño marinade frighten you away; this dish has just the right amount of heat. If you have the time, you can marinate the beef in the refrigerator up to a day in advance. Otherwise, mix it with the seasonings just before cooking; the flavor will still be deliciously spicy and savory.

1 fresh jalapeño or other small fresh hot chile, seeded and minced

2 cloves garlic, minced or pressed

¼ to ½ teaspoon ground red pepper (cayenne)

1 tablespoon (15 ml) reduced-sodium soy sauce

½ teaspoon sugar

1 pound (455 g) lean boneless top sirloin steak (about 1 inch/2.5 cm thick), trimmed of fat and cut across the grain into ⅛- by 2-inch (3-mm by 5-cm) strips

4 to 8 low-fat flour tortillas (*each* 7 to 9 inches/18 to 23 cm in diameter)

1 large onion, thinly sliced

1 teaspoon olive oil

Condiments (suggestions follow)

In a large bowl, stir together chile, garlic, red pepper, soy sauce, and sugar. Add steak and stir to coat. Set aside.

Brush tortillas lightly with hot water; then stack, wrap in foil, and heat in a 350°F/175°C oven until warm (10 to 12 minutes).

Meanwhile, in a wide nonstick frying pan or wok, combine onion and ¼ cup (60 ml) water. Stir-fry over medium-high heat until onion is soft and liquid has evaporated (4 to 5 minutes). Add oil; then stir in meat and its marinade. Stir-fry until meat is done to your liking; cut to test (2 to 3 minutes for rare).

To serve, spoon meat mixture into tortillas; offer condiments to add to taste. Makes 4 servings.

Condiments. In individual bowls, offer 3 or more of the following: shredded **lettuce,** chopped **tomatoes, Tomatillo-Lime Salsa** (page 55) or purchased salsa, **nonfat sour cream, cilantro leaves,** and **lime wedges.**

Per serving: 293 calories (20% calories from fat), 28 g protein, 34 g carbohydrates, 7 g total fat (2 g saturated fat), 69 mg cholesterol, 488 mg sodium

Jamaican Jerk Beef with Spiced Rice

Preparation time: About 15 minutes, plus at least 30 minutes to marinate meat
Cooking time: About 30 minutes

•

Bound to win raves from spicy-food lovers, this memorable dish is a perfect choice for cold winter nights. A complex seasoning paste flavors both the beef and the currant-dotted rice that's served alongside.

Jerk Seasoning Paste (recipe follows)

1 pound (455 g) lean boneless top sirloin steak (about 1 inch/2.5 cm thick), trimmed of fat and cut across the grain into ⅛- by 2-inch (3-mm by 5-cm) strips

2 cups (470 ml) fat-free reduced-sodium chicken broth

¼ cup (60 ml) half-and-half

1 cup (185 g) long-grain white rice

¼ cup (35 g) dried currants or raisins

1 teaspoon olive oil

Cilantro sprigs

Lime wedges

Prepare Jerk Seasoning Paste. Measure out 1 tablespoon of the paste; cover and set aside. Place remaining paste in a large bowl; add steak and turn or stir to coat. Cover and refrigerate for at least 30 minutes or until next day, stirring occasionally.

Meanwhile, in a 2- to 3-quart (1.9- to 2.8-liter) pan, combine broth, half-and-half, and the reserved 1 tablespoon seasoning paste. Bring just to a boil over medium-high heat, stirring; then stir in rice and currants. Reduce heat, cover, and simmer until liquid has been absorbed and rice is tender to bite (about 20 minutes). Spoon rice mixture onto a rimmed platter and keep warm.

Heat oil in a wide nonstick frying pan or wok over medium-high heat. When oil is hot, add meat and stir-fry

Continued on next page

Jamaican Jerk Beef with Spiced Rice (continued)

until done to your liking; cut to test (2 to 3 minutes for rare). Spoon meat over rice; garnish with cilantro sprigs. Serve with lime wedges. Makes 4 servings.

Jerk Seasoning Paste. In a blender or food processor, combine ¼ cup (10 g) firmly packed **cilantro leaves,** 3 tablespoons minced **fresh ginger,** 3 tablespoons (45 ml) **water,** 2 tablespoons **whole black peppercorns,** 1 tablespoon *each* **ground allspice** and firmly packed **brown sugar,** 2 cloves **garlic** (peeled), ½ teaspoon **crushed red pepper flakes,** and ¼ teaspoon *each* **ground coriander** and **ground nutmeg.** Whirl until smooth. If made ahead, cover and refrigerate for up to 2 days.

Per serving: 412 calories (19% calories from fat), 31 g protein, 53 g carbohydrates, 9 g total fat (3 g saturated fat), 75 mg cholesterol, 403 mg sodium

Sweet & Sour Pork

Pictured on facing page
Preparation time: About 25 minutes
Cooking time: About 15 minutes

•

All the classic ingredients are here—tender pork, crisp bell pepper and onion, juicy pineapple chunks, and a tart-sweet sauce—but this rendition of sweet and sour pork is far lower in fat than most traditional recipes. To streamline this long-time favorite, we use lean pork tenderloin, then stir-fry the meat in a light batter, using a minimum of oil.

> Sweet-Sour Sauce (recipe follows)
> 1   large egg white
> ⅓   cup (45 g) cornstarch
> 1   pound (455 g) pork tenderloin, trimmed of fat and cut into 1-inch (2.5-cm) chunks

> 1   tablespoon (15 ml) salad oil
> 1   large onion, cut into thin wedges
> 1   large green bell pepper (about 8 oz./230 g), seeded and cut into 1-inch (2.5-cm) squares
> 1   or 2 cloves garlic, minced or pressed
> 1   large tomato (about 8 oz./230 g), cut into wedges
> 1½   cups (235 g) fresh or canned pineapple chunks, drained

Prepare Sweet-Sour Sauce and set aside.

In a medium-size bowl, beat egg white to blend well. Place cornstarch in another medium-size bowl. Dip pork chunks, a portion at a time, in egg white; then coat lightly with cornstarch and shake off excess.

Heat oil in a wide nonstick frying pan or wok over medium-high heat. When oil is hot, add meat and stir-fry gently until golden brown on outside and no longer pink in center; cut to test (about 8 minutes). Add water, 1 tablespoon (15 ml) at a time, if pan appears dry. Remove meat from pan with a slotted spoon; keep warm.

Add onion, bell pepper, garlic, and 1 tablespoon (15 ml) water to pan; stir-fry for 1 minute. Add more water, 1 tablespoon (15 ml) at a time, if pan appears dry. Stir Sweet-Sour Sauce well and pour into pan. Cook, stirring, until sauce boils and thickens slightly (2 to 3 minutes).

Add tomato, pineapple, and meat to pan. Cook, stirring gently, just until heated through (1 to 2 minutes). Makes 4 servings.

Sweet-Sour Sauce. In a medium-size bowl, stir together 4 teaspoons **cornstarch** and ¼ cup (60 ml) **white wine vinegar** or distilled white vinegar until blended. Then stir in ¾ cup (180 ml) **water,** ¼ cup (50 g) **sugar,** 1 tablespoon (15 ml) *each* **catsup** and **reduced-sodium soy sauce,** and ⅛ teaspoon **Hot Chili Oil** (page 69) or purchased hot chili oil, or to taste.

Per serving: 355 calories (20% calories from fat), 27 g protein, 45 g carbohydrates, 8 g total fat (2 g saturated fat), 74 mg cholesterol, 275 mg sodium

· ·

Flavorful Sweet & Sour Pork (recipe at left) is a perfect main course for a lean Chinese-style meal. Spice up each serving with homemade Hot Chili Oil (recipe on page 69), if you like.

Island Pork with Coconut Couscous

Preparation time: About 25 minutes
Cooking time: About 15 minutes

•

To make couscous and rice seem richer, try cooking them in low-fat milk—or in a combination of broth and milk, as we do here. The creamy-tasting couscous, sweetened with a little shredded coconut, accompanies luscious sliced mangoes and a ginger-seasoned stir-fry of pork tenderloin and bright bell pepper.

- 2 or 3 large mangoes (1½ to 2¼ lbs./680 g to 1.02 kg *total*)
- 1 to 2 tablespoons (15 to 30 ml) lime juice
  Cooking Sauce (recipe follows)
- 1 cup (240 ml) fat-free reduced-sodium chicken broth
- ⅔ cup (160 ml) low-fat milk
- 1 cup (185 g) couscous
- ¼ cup (20 g) sweetened shredded coconut
- 2 teaspoons olive oil
- 1 tablespoon minced fresh ginger
- 2 cloves garlic, minced or pressed
- 1 pound (455 g) pork tenderloin, trimmed of fat and cut into 1-inch (2.5-cm) chunks
- 1 large red or green bell pepper (about 8 oz./230 g), seeded and cut into thin strips
- ¼ cup (25 g) thinly sliced green onions
  Lime wedges

Peel mangoes; cut fruit from pits in thin slices and place in a large bowl. Add lime juice (use 2 tablespoons/30 ml juice if using 3 mangoes) and mix gently to coat. Arrange mangoes attractively on 4 individual plates; cover and set aside. Prepare Cooking Sauce and set aside.

In a 3- to 4-quart (2.8- to 3.8-liter) pan, bring broth and milk just to a boil over medium-high heat; stir in couscous. Cover, remove from heat, and let stand until liquid has been absorbed (about 5 minutes). Stir in coconut. Keep warm; fluff occasionally with a fork.

Heat oil in a wide nonstick frying pan or wok over medium-high heat. When oil is hot, add ginger and gar-

lic; stir-fry just until fragrant (about 30 seconds; do not scorch). Add pork and stir-fry until lightly browned on outside and no longer pink in center; cut to test (about 8 minutes). Add water, 1 tablespoon (15 ml) at a time, if pan appears dry. Remove meat from pan with a slotted spoon; keep warm.

Add bell pepper and 2 tablespoons (30 ml) water to pan. Stir-fry until bell pepper is just tender-crisp to bite (about 2 minutes); add water, 1 tablespoon (15 ml) at a time, if pan appears dry. Stir Cooking Sauce well and pour into pan. Cook, stirring, until sauce boils and thickens slightly (1 to 2 minutes). Remove pan from heat and add meat and onions; mix gently but thoroughly.

Spoon couscous alongside mango slices; spoon meat mixture alongside couscous. Serve with lime wedges. Makes 4 servings.

Cooking Sauce. Place 1 tablespoon **cornstarch** in a small bowl. Gradually add ¾ cup (180 ml) **mango or pear nectar,** stirring until cornstarch is smoothly dissolved. Stir in 1½ teaspoons **Oriental sesame oil** and ¼ teaspoon **salt.**

Per serving: 541 calories (18% calories from fat), 33 g protein, 79 g carbohydrates, 11 g total fat (4 g saturated fat), 77 mg cholesterol, 398 mg sodium

Sausage, Basil & Port Fettuccine

Preparation time: About 20 minutes
Cooking time: About 25 minutes

•

Red and green onions simmered in port make a superb base for a rich sausage-tomato sauce to serve over tender fettuccine.

- 1 pound (455 g) mild or hot pork Italian sausages (casings removed), crumbled into ½-inch (1-cm) pieces
- 2 cloves garlic, minced or pressed
- 1½ cups (150 g) sliced green onions
- 3 cups (345 g) thinly sliced red onions
- 1½ cups (240 ml) port

3 medium-size tomatoes (about 1¼ lbs./565 g *total*), chopped

2 tablespoons (30 ml) balsamic vinegar

¾ cup (30 g) chopped fresh basil

1 pound (455 g) dried fettuccine

 Basil sprigs

In a wide nonstick frying pan or wok, stir-fry sausage over medium-high heat until browned (7 to 10 minutes). Remove from pan with a slotted spoon; keep warm. Pour off and discard all but 1 teaspoon fat from pan.

Add garlic, green onions, and red onions to pan and stir-fry until soft (5 to 7 minutes). Add water, 1 table-spoon (15 ml) at a time, if pan appears dry. Add port and bring to a boil. Then boil, stirring often, until liquid is reduced by half (5 to 6 minutes). Add tomatoes, vinegar, and sausage; reduce heat and simmer for 2 minutes. Stir in chopped basil.

While sauce is cooking, in a 6- to 8-quart (6- to 8-liter) pan, cook fettuccine in about 4 quarts (3.8 liters) boiling water until just tender to bite (8 to 10 minutes); or cook according to package directions.

Drain pasta well and transfer to a warm wide bowl; top with sausage sauce. Garnish with basil sprigs. Makes 8 servings.

Per serving: 473 calories (29% calories from fat), 18 g protein, 58 g carbohydrates, 14 g total fat (4 g saturated fat), 87 mg cholesterol, 417 mg sodium

Gingered Pork with Asian Pears

Preparation time: About 15 minutes
Cooking time: About 20 minutes

●

Round, crisp Asian pears—sometimes called "apple pears"—make a mild, slightly sweet foil for stir-fried pork chunks. If you can't find Asian pears, use your favorite regular variety; Bartlett and Anjou are both good.

3 large firm-ripe Asian or regular pears (about 1½ lbs./680 g *total*), peeled, cored, and thinly sliced

3 tablespoons (45 ml) cider vinegar

1 teaspoon salad oil

1 pound (455 g) pork tenderloin, trimmed of fat and cut into 1-inch (2.5-cm) chunks

2 tablespoons firmly packed brown sugar

⅔ cup (160 ml) *each* dry white wine and fat-free reduced-sodium chicken broth

2 teaspoons minced fresh ginger

4 teaspoons cornstarch blended with 4 teaspoons cold water

½ to ¾ cup (15 to 23 g) finely shredded spinach

In a large bowl, gently mix pears and 1 tablespoon (15 ml) of the vinegar. Set aside.

Heat oil in a wide nonstick frying pan or wok over medium-high heat. When oil is hot, add pork and stir-fry until lightly browned on outside and no longer pink in center; cut to test (about 8 minutes). Add water, 1 tablespoon (15 ml) at a time, if pan appears dry. Remove meat from pan with a slotted spoon; keep warm.

Add sugar and remaining 2 tablespoons (30 ml) vinegar to pan. Bring to a boil; then boil, stirring, for 1 minute. Add wine, broth, and ginger; return to a boil. Boil, stirring, for 3 minutes. Add pears and cook, gently turning pears often, until pears are heated through (about 3 minutes). Stir cornstarch mixture well and pour into pan. Cook, stirring, until sauce boils and thickens slightly (1 to 2 minutes).

Remove pan from heat; return meat to pan and mix gently but thoroughly. Gently stir in spinach. Makes 4 servings.

Per serving: 309 calories (18% calories from fat), 25 g protein, 34 g carbohydrates, 6 g total fat (2 g saturated fat), 74 mg cholesterol, 177 mg sodium

Meatless Main Dishes

*F*or superb meatless meals that are low in fat, focus on pasta, grains, tofu, and beans in variety. Served in combination—as in Sweet & Sour Tofu or Sautéed Bean Burritos—these foods provide great nutrition and supremely satisfying dining, too.

....

Capellini with Cilantro Pesto & White Beans (recipe on page 80) makes a striking entrée. A delicious blend of warm tomatoes and creamy-textured beans is served over delicate angel hair pasta and a bright herb pesto.

Capellini with Cilantro Pesto & White Beans

Pictured on page 78
Preparation time: About 20 minutes
Cooking time: About 15 minutes

•

To make this pretty layered dish, you spread a vivid cilantro pesto on each plate, then top with angel hair pasta and a sauce of mild cannellini beans and diced tomatoes. Because the pesto is based on water rather than oil, it may weep a bit on standing—so be sure to stir it well before using it.

 Cilantro Pesto (recipe follows)

8 ounces (230 g) dried capellini

2 tablespoons (30 ml) seasoned rice vinegar (or 2 tablespoons/30 ml distilled white vinegar plus ¾ teaspoon sugar)

1 medium-size red onion, cut into thin slivers

1 tablespoon (15 ml) balsamic vinegar

1 can (about 15 oz./430 g) cannellini (white kidney beans), drained and rinsed

7 medium-size firm-ripe pear-shaped (Roma-type) tomatoes (about 1 lb./455 g *total*), chopped

1½ teaspoons chopped fresh thyme or ½ teaspoon dried thyme

 Thyme and cilantro sprigs

 Pepper

Prepare Cilantro Pesto and set aside.

 In a 4- to 5-quart (3.8- to 5-liter) pan, cook capellini in about 8 cups (1.9 liters) boiling water until just tender to bite (about 3 minutes); or cook according to package directions. Drain well, rinse with hot water, and drain well again. Quickly return pasta to pan; add rice vinegar and lift with 2 forks to mix. Keep warm.

 While pasta is cooking, combine onion and ⅓ cup (80 ml) water in a wide nonstick frying pan or wok. Cover and cook over medium-high heat until onion is almost soft (about 3 minutes). Uncover, add balsamic vinegar, and stir-fry until liquid has evaporated. Add beans, tomatoes, and chopped thyme to pan; stir-fry gently until beans are heated through and tomatoes are soft (about 3 minutes). Remove pan from heat.

 Stir Cilantro Pesto well; spread evenly on 4 individual plates. Top with pasta, then with bean mixture. Garnish with thyme and cilantro sprigs; serve immediately. Season to taste with pepper. Makes 4 servings.

Cilantro Pesto. In a blender or food processor, combine 3 cups (120 g) firmly packed **cilantro leaves**, 1 cup (about 3 oz./85 g) grated **Parmesan cheese**, ½ cup (120 ml) **water**, 1 tablespoon **grated lemon peel**, 1 tablespoon (15 ml) **Oriental sesame oil**, 3 cloves **garlic** (peeled), and 2 teaspoons **honey**. Whirl until smoothly puréed. If pesto is too thick, add a little more **water**. If made ahead, cover and refrigerate for up to 3 hours; bring to room temperature before using.

Per serving: 473 calories (21% calories from fat), 20 g protein, 73 g carbohydrates, 11 g total fat (4 g saturated fat), 16 mg cholesterol, 786 mg sodium

Sautéed Bean Burritos

Preparation time: About 20 minutes
Cooking time: About 15 minutes

•

Jalapeño jack cheese adds just the right amount of heat to burritos filled with a quick sauté of pinto beans and crisp, sweet yellow or white corn.

 Cooking Sauce (recipe follows)

8 low-fat flour tortillas (*each* 7 to 9 inches/18 to 23 cm in diameter)

1 teaspoon salad oil

1 large onion, chopped

1 medium-size red or green bell pepper (about 6 oz./170 g), seeded and diced

1 can (about 15 oz./430 g) pinto or kidney beans, drained and rinsed

 About 1½ cups (250 g) cooked fresh corn kernels (from 2 small ears yellow or white corn); or 1 package (about 10 oz./285 g) frozen corn kernels, thawed and drained

1 cup (about 4 oz./115 g) shredded jalapeño or regular jack cheese

½ cup (20 g) lightly packed cilantro leaves

½ to 1 cup (120 to 240 ml) nonfat sour cream

Prepare Cooking Sauce and set aside. Brush tortillas lightly with hot water; then stack, wrap in foil, and heat in a 350°F/175°C oven until warm (10 to 12 minutes).

Meanwhile, heat oil in a wide nonstick frying pan or wok over medium-high heat. When oil is hot, add onion, bell pepper, and 2 tablespoons (30 ml) water; stir-fry until onion is soft (about 5 minutes). Add more water, 1 tablespoon (15 ml) at a time, if pan appears dry. Add beans and corn; stir-fry gently until heated through (about 3 minutes). Stir Cooking Sauce well and pour into pan. Cook, stirring gently, until sauce boils and thickens slightly (1 to 2 minutes).

Top tortillas equally with bean mixture. Sprinkle with cheese and cilantro, top with sour cream, and roll to enclose; eat out of hand. Makes 4 servings.

Cooking Sauce. In a small bowl, stir together 1 teaspoon **water** and ½ teaspoon **cornstarch** until blended. Then stir in ½ teaspoon **grated lime peel,** 2 tablespoons (30 ml) **lime juice,** 1 teaspoon **honey,** ½ teaspoon **ground coriander,** and ¼ teaspoon **ground cumin.**

Per serving: 459 calories (23% calories from fat), 21 g protein, 75 g carbohydrates, 13 g total fat (5 g saturated fat), 30 mg cholesterol, 766 mg sodium

---

Swiss Chard with Garbanzos & Parmesan

Preparation time: About 20 minutes
Cooking time: About 20 minutes

•

Swiss chard tastes something like spinach—and like spinach, it's leafy, deep green, and rich in vitamin A and iron. Here, the slivered leaves are sautéed with onions and a little lemon peel, then topped with nutty garbanzo beans and tomatoes for a satisfying supper dish. Serve with a crusty whole wheat loaf and a fresh fruit salad.

3   **tablespoons (45 ml) molasses**

1½ **teaspoons dry mustard**

1½ **teaspoons Worcestershire or reduced-sodium soy sauce**

¾   **teaspoon chopped fresh oregano or ¼ teaspoon dried oregano**

1   **pound (455 g) Swiss chard**

1   **teaspoon olive oil**

2   **large onions, thinly sliced**

½   **teaspoon grated lemon peel**
    Salt

2   **large tomatoes (about 1 lb./455 g** *total***), chopped**

1   **can (about 15 oz./430 g) garbanzo beans, drained and rinsed**

1   **teaspoon cornstarch blended with 1 teaspoon cold water**

½   **cup (43 g) shredded Parmesan cheese**
    Oregano sprigs

In a small bowl, stir together molasses, mustard, Worcestershire, and chopped oregano. Set aside.

Trim and discard discolored stem ends from chard; then rinse chard, drain, and cut crosswise into ½-inch (1-cm) strips. Set aside.

Heat oil in a wide nonstick frying pan or wok over medium-high heat. When oil is hot, add onions, lemon peel, and 2 tablespoons (30 ml) water. Stir-fry until onions are soft (about 7 minutes). Add water, 1 tablespoon (15 ml) at a time, if pan appears dry. Add half the chard and 1 tablespoon (15 ml) more water to pan; stir-fry until chard just begins to wilt. Then add remaining chard and 1 tablespoon (15 ml) more water; stir-fry until all chard is wilted and bright green (3 to 4 more minutes). Season to taste with salt. Spoon chard mixture around edge of a rimmed platter and keep warm.

Stir molasses mixture and pour into pan; add tomatoes and beans. Stir-fry gently until beans are heated through and tomatoes are soft (about 3 minutes). Stir cornstarch mixture well and pour into pan. Cook, stirring gently, until mixture boils and thickens slightly (1 to 2 minutes).

Spoon bean mixture into center of platter; sprinkle cheese over all. Garnish with oregano sprigs. Makes 4 servings.

Per serving: 264 calories (22% calories from fat), 12 g protein, 42 g carbohydrates, 7 g total fat (2 g saturated fat), 8 mg cholesterol, 566 mg sodium

Stir-fried Broccoli, Garlic & Beans

Pictured on facing page
Preparation time: About 25 minutes
Cooking time: About 30 minutes

•

Broccoli, earthy-tasting black beans, and plenty of garlic go into this Asian-inspired stir-fry. Start the shiitake mushrooms soaking first; while they stand, you can cook the rice and do most of the other preparation.

  1 **package (about ½ oz./15 g) dried shiitake mushrooms**

  1 **cup (185 g) long-grain white rice**

  1 **medium-size head garlic (about 3 oz./85 g)**

  2 **teaspoons salad oil**

  5 **cups (355 g) broccoli flowerets**

  1 **can (about 15 oz./430 g) black beans, drained and rinsed**

  2 **tablespoons (30 ml) reduced-sodium soy sauce**

  1 **teaspoon Oriental sesame oil**

  ½ **teaspoon honey**

Soak mushrooms in hot water to cover until soft and pliable (about 20 minutes). Rub mushrooms gently to release any grit; then lift mushrooms from water. Discard water. Squeeze mushrooms gently to remove moisture; trim and discard tough stems. Thinly slice caps, place in a small bowl, and set aside.

While mushrooms are soaking, in a 3- to 4-quart (2.8- to 3.8-liter) pan, bring 2 cups (470 ml) water to a boil over high heat; stir in rice. Reduce heat, cover, and simmer until liquid has been absorbed and rice is tender to bite (about 20 minutes). Transfer to a rimmed platter and keep warm. Fluff occasionally with a fork.

Separate garlic into cloves; then peel and thinly slice garlic cloves. Heat salad oil in a wide nonstick frying pan or wok over medium-high heat. When oil is hot, add garlic and stir-fry gently just until tinged with brown (about 2 minutes; do not scorch). Add water, 1 tablespoon (15 ml) at a time, if pan appears dry. Remove garlic from pan with a slotted spoon; place in bowl with mushrooms.

Add broccoli and ⅓ cup (80 ml) water to pan. Cover and cook until broccoli is almost tender-crisp to bite

(about 3 minutes). Uncover and stir-fry until liquid has evaporated. Add beans and stir-fry gently until heated through. Remove from heat and add mushroom mixture, soy sauce, sesame oil, and honey; mix gently but thoroughly. Spoon broccoli mixture over rice. Makes 4 servings.

Per serving: 352 calories (12% calories from fat), 15 g protein, 66 g carbohydrates, 5 g total fat (0.6 g saturated fat), 0 mg cholesterol, 516 mg sodium

Vegetable-Bean Chili

Preparation time: About 15 minutes
Cooking time: About 15 minutes

•

This colorful chili is quite mild in flavor. If you prefer more heat, use more chili powder and be generous with the red pepper flakes. We call for Worcestershire as a seasoning, but since it's made with anchovies (or other fish), strict vegetarians will want to use soy sauce instead.

  3 **tablespoons (45 ml) molasses**

  1½ **teaspoons dry mustard**

  1½ **teaspoons Worcestershire or reduced-sodium soy sauce**

  1 **teaspoon olive oil or salad oil**

  2 **cloves garlic, minced or pressed**

  2 **medium-size carrots (about 8 oz./230 g total), cut into ¼-inch (6-mm) slanting slices**

  1 **large onion, chopped**

  1 **tablespoon chili powder, or to taste**

  2 or 3 **large tomatoes (1 to 1½ lbs./455 to 680 g total), chopped**

  1 **can (about 15 oz./430 g) *each* pinto beans and red kidney beans, drained and rinsed**

  About ½ cup (120 ml) plain nonfat yogurt

  Crushed red pepper flakes

Continued on page 84

•••••••••••••••••••••••••••••••••••••••

Savor one of the world's favorite seasonings—and lots of it!—in colorful Stir-fried Broccoli, Garlic & Beans (recipe at left). Spooned over hot rice, the dish makes a satisfying, surprisingly rich-tasting meal.

Vegetable-Bean Chili (continued)

In a small bowl, stir together molasses, mustard, and Worcestershire. Set aside.

Heat oil in a wide nonstick frying pan or wok over medium-high heat. When oil is hot, add garlic and stir-fry just until fragrant (about 30 seconds; do not scorch). Add carrots, onion, chili powder, and ¼ cup (60 ml) water. Cover and cook until carrots are almost tender to bite (about 4 minutes). Uncover and stir-fry until liquid has evaporated.

Stir molasses mixture and pour into pan; then add tomatoes and beans. Stir-fry gently until beans are heated through and tomatoes are soft (3 to 5 minutes). Ladle chili into bowls and top with yogurt. Season to taste with red pepper flakes. Makes 4 servings.

Per serving: 290 calories (10% calories from fat), 14 g protein, 54 g carbohydrates, 3 g total fat (0.3 g saturated fat), 0.6 mg cholesterol, 405 mg sodium

Couscous Bean Paella

Preparation time: About 15 minutes
Cooking time: About 15 minutes

•

Like many traditional paellas, this meatless version calls for sweet peppers, green peas, artichokes, and saffron—but it's made with quick-cooking couscous, not rice, and the protein comes from black beans rather than chicken and shellfish. Serve it with a warm sourdough loaf and crisp greens tossed with a light vinaigrette.

　2　teaspoons olive oil
　1　large onion, chopped
　1　medium-size red bell pepper (about 6 oz./170 g), seeded and cut into ½-inch (1-cm) squares
2¼　cups (590 ml) canned vegetable broth
　⅛　teaspoon saffron threads, or to taste
　1　package (about 9 oz./255 g) frozen artichoke hearts, thawed and drained
　1　cup (145 g) frozen peas, thawed and drained
1½　cups (275 g) couscous
　1　can (about 15 oz./430 g) black beans, drained and rinsed
　　Lime or lemon wedges

Heat oil in a wide nonstick frying pan or wok over medium-high heat. When oil is hot, add onion, bell pepper, and ¼ cup (60 ml) water. Stir-fry until onion is soft (about 5 minutes); add water, 1 tablespoon (15 ml) at a time, if pan appears dry.

Add broth, saffron, artichokes, and peas to pan. Bring to a rolling boil. Stir in couscous. Cover pan, remove from heat, and let stand until liquid has been absorbed (about 5 minutes). Gently stir in beans; cover and let stand for 2 to 3 minutes to heat beans. Serve with lime wedges. Makes 4 servings.

Per serving: 429 calories (9% calories from fat), 17 g protein, 83 g carbohydrates, 4 g total fat (0.5 g saturated fat), 0 mg cholesterol, 1,379 mg sodium

Sichuan Tofu with Eggplant

Preparation time: About 30 minutes, plus at least 1 hour to soak Green Onion Brushes (if used)
Cooking time: About 15 minutes

•

Though it's based on two exceptionally mild-flavored foods—tofu and eggplant—this dish will nonetheless win favor with the fire-eaters in your family. Fresh ginger and bottled chili paste with garlic make it spicy.

　　Green Onion Brushes (optional; directions follow)
　　Cooking Sauce (recipe follows)
　　About 1 pound (455 g) firm tofu, rinsed, drained, and cut into ½-inch (1-cm) cubes
　10　**ounces (285 g) fresh Chinese noodles or linguine**
　1　**tablespoon (15 ml) salad oil**
　2　**medium-size eggplants (about 1½ lbs./680 g *total*), peeled and cut into ½-inch (1-cm) pieces (about 8 cups)**
　2　**teaspoons minced fresh ginger**
　2　**green onions, thinly sliced**
　½　**cup (20 g) lightly packed cilantro leaves**

Prepare Green Onion Brushes, if desired. Prepare Cooking Sauce. Add tofu to sauce and stir gently to coat; set aside.

In a 5- to 6-quart (5- to 6-liter) pan, cook noodles in about 3 quarts (2.8 liters) boiling water until just tender to bite (3 to 5 minutes); or cook according to package directions. Drain well, transfer to a warm rimmed platter, and keep warm.

While noodles are cooking, heat oil in a wide nonstick frying pan or wok over medium-high heat. Add eggplant and ¼ cup (60 ml) water. Stir-fry until eggplant is soft and tinged with gold (8 to 10 minutes); add more water, 1 tablespoon (15 ml) at a time, if pan appears dry. Add ginger and stir-fry just until fragrant (about 30 seconds; do not scorch). Add tofu mixture and cook, stirring gently, until sauce boils and tofu is heated through (about 3 minutes). Remove from heat and stir in sliced onions.

Spoon tofu mixture over noodles and sprinkle with cilantro. Garnish with Green Onion Brushes, if desired. Makes 4 to 6 servings.

Green Onion Brushes. Cut the white part of 3 to 5 **green onions** into 1½-inch (3.5-cm) lengths. Using scissors or a sharp knife, slash both ends of each onion piece lengthwise 3 or 4 times, making cuts about ½ inch (1 cm) deep. Place onions in a bowl, cover with **ice water,** and refrigerate until ends curl (at least 1 hour) or for up to 8 hours.

Cooking Sauce. In a large bowl, stir together 3 tablespoons (45 ml) **hoisin sauce,** 2 tablespoons (30 ml) **seasoned rice vinegar** (or 2 tablespoons/30 ml distilled white vinegar plus ¾ teaspoon sugar), 1 tablespoon *each* **sugar** and **chili paste with garlic,** and 2 teaspoons **Oriental sesame oil.**

Per serving: 476 calories (30% calories from fat), 24 g protein, 62 g carbohydrates, 16 g total fat (2 g saturated fat), 54 mg cholesterol, 351 mg sodium

Sautéed Tofu with Black Bean & Corn Salsa

Preparation time: About 20 minutes
Cooking time: About 15 minutes

●

Besides its delicious tangy-spicy-sweet flavor, this dish offers great contrasts of color and texture. Crisp red bell pepper and yellow corn are combined with shiny black beans, then topped with lightly seasoned tofu to make a satisfying lunch or dinner.

> 1 **pound (455 g) firm tofu, rinsed, drained, and cut into ½-inch (1-cm) cubes**
> 1 **teaspoon chili powder**
> ¼ **teaspoon salt**
> ½ **teaspoon grated lime peel**
> 2 **tablespoons (30 ml) lime juice**
> 2 **teaspoons honey**
> ¾ **teaspoon ground cumin**
> 1 **large onion, chopped**
> 1 **medium-size red bell pepper (about 6 oz./170 g), seeded and chopped**
> 1 **can (about 15 oz./430 g) black beans, drained and rinsed**
> 1 **package (about 10 oz./285 g) frozen corn kernels, thawed and drained**
> 1 **teaspoon olive oil**
> 1 **or 2 cloves garlic, minced or pressed**
> ¼ **cup (10 g) lightly packed cilantro leaves**
> **Lime wedges**

In a large bowl, gently mix tofu, chili powder, and salt; set aside. In a small bowl, stir together lime peel, lime juice, honey, and cumin; set aside.

In a wide nonstick frying pan or wok, combine onion, bell pepper, and ¼ cup (60 ml) water. Stir-fry over medium-high heat until onion is soft (about 5 minutes). Add beans, corn, and lime juice mixture; stir-fry gently until beans and corn are heated through (about 3 minutes). Remove bean mixture from pan and keep warm. Wipe pan clean (be careful; pan is hot).

Heat oil in pan over medium-high heat. When oil is hot, add tofu and garlic. Stir-fry gently until tofu is heated through (3 to 4 minutes); add water, 1 tablespoon (15 ml) at a time, if pan appears dry.

Divide bean mixture among 4 individual plates; top equally with tofu. Sprinkle with cilantro and garnish with lime wedges. Makes 4 servings.

Per serving: 345 calories (30% calories from fat), 25 g protein, 41 g carbohydrates, 12 g total fat (2 g saturated fat), 0 mg cholesterol, 200 mg sodium

Tofu Tacos with Pineapple Salsa

Pictured on facing page
Preparation time: About 15 minutes
Cooking time: About 20 minutes

•

Definitely not your standard tacos, these tofu-topped soft tortillas are sure to appeal to the vegetarian crowd. The filling is a colorful combination of bell pepper, corn kernels, and teriyaki-seasoned tofu; a crunchy pineapple-jicama salsa adds a refreshing accent. You can make the flavored oils used in the marinade yourself (see pages 68 and 69) or use purchased equivalents.

3 tablespoons (45 ml) reduced-sodium soy sauce

2 tablespoons (30 ml) honey

1 tablespoon (15 ml) Basil Oil (page 68) or purchased basil oil (or 1 tablespoon salad oil plus ½ teaspoon dried basil)

1 teaspoon Hot Chili Oil (page 69) or purchased hot chili oil

2 cloves garlic, minced or pressed

12 ounces (340 g) firm tofu, rinsed, drained, and cut into ½-inch (1-cm) cubes

   Pineapple Salsa (recipe follows)

4 low-fat flour tortillas (*each* 7 to 9 inches/18 to 23 cm in diameter)

1 large red bell pepper (about 8 oz./230 g), seeded and finely chopped

1 large onion, finely chopped

1 package (about 10 oz./285 g) frozen corn kernels, thawed and drained

In a medium-size bowl, stir together soy sauce, honey, Basil Oil, Hot Chili Oil, and garlic. Add tofu and stir gently to coat. Set aside; stir occasionally. Prepare Pineapple Salsa and set aside.

···

Irresistibly spicy, Tofu Tacos with Pineapple Salsa (recipe above) provide a delicious way to get high-protein tofu on the menu. Accompany the tacos with a vegetable platter and your favorite iced beverage.

Brush tortillas lightly with hot water; then stack tortillas, wrap in foil, and heat in a 350°F/175°C oven until warm (10 to 12 minutes).

Meanwhile, in a wide nonstick frying pan or wok, combine tofu (and any marinade), bell pepper, and onion. Stir-fry gently over medium-high heat until tofu is browned (about 15 minutes). Add water, 1 tablespoon (15 ml) at a time, if pan appears dry. Add corn and stir-fry until heated through.

Top tortillas equally with tofu mixture and Pineapple Salsa; roll up and eat out of hand. Makes 4 servings.

Pineapple Salsa. In a large bowl, mix 1 cup (155 g) diced **fresh or canned pineapple;** ½ cup (65 g) peeled, shredded **jicama;** 1 teaspoon **grated lime peel;** 3 tablespoons (45 ml) **lime juice;** and 2 tablespoons minced **fresh basil.**

Per serving: 411 calories (30% calories from fat), 20 g protein, 57 g carbohydrates, 15 g total fat (2 g saturated fat), 0 mg cholesterol, 761 mg sodium

Sweet & Sour Tofu

Preparation time: About 15 minutes
Cooking time: About 25 minutes

•

The tempting, chili-spiked sweet-sour sauce we use on juicy pork chunks (see page 74) is just as good with tender tofu and crunchy, quick-cooked red onion and bell pepper. Hot, fluffy rice is a must with this beautiful dish—it's essential for soaking up the sauce!

1 cup (185 g) long-grain white rice

   Sweet-Sour Sauce (recipe follows)

1 pound (455 g) firm tofu, rinsed, drained, and cut into ½-inch (1-cm) cubes

1 teaspoon paprika

1 or 2 cloves garlic, minced or pressed

¼ teaspoon salt

1 teaspoon salad oil

1 small red onion, cut into thin wedges

1 large green, red, or yellow bell pepper (about

Continued on next page

Sweet & Sour Tofu (continued)

    8 oz./230 g), seeded and cut into 1-inch (2.5-cm) squares

  1 medium-size tomato (about 6 oz./170 g), cut into thin wedges

1½ cups (235 g) fresh or canned pineapple chunks, drained

In a 3- to 4-quart (2.8- to 3.8-liter) pan, bring 2 cups (470 ml) water to a boil over high heat; stir in rice. Reduce heat, cover, and simmer until liquid has been absorbed and rice is tender to bite (about 20 minutes).

Meanwhile, prepare Sweet-Sour Sauce and set aside. In a large bowl, gently mix tofu, paprika, garlic, and salt; set aside.

Heat oil in a wide nonstick frying pan or wok over medium-high heat. When oil is hot, add tofu and stir-fry gently until heated through (3 to 4 minutes). Add water, 1 tablespoon (15 ml) at a time, if pan appears dry. Remove tofu from pan with a slotted spoon; keep warm.

Add onion, bell pepper, and 2 tablespoons (30 ml) water to pan. Stir-fry for 1 minute; add water, 1 tablespoon (15 ml) at a time, if pan appears dry. Stir Sweet-Sour Sauce well; pour into pan. Cook, stirring, until sauce boils and thickens slightly (2 to 3 minutes). Stir in tomato, pineapple, and tofu; stir gently just until heated through (about 2 minutes).

To serve, spoon rice onto a rimmed platter; top with tofu mixture. Makes 4 servings.

Sweet-Sour Sauce. In a medium-size bowl, stir together 4 teaspoons **cornstarch** and ¼ cup (60 ml) **white wine vinegar** or distilled white vinegar until blended. Then stir in ¾ cup (180 ml) **water**, ¼ cup (50 g) **sugar,** 1 tablespoon (15 ml) *each* **catsup** and **reduced-sodium soy sauce,** and ⅛ teaspoon **Hot Chili Oil** (page 69) or purchased hot chili oil, or to taste.

Per serving: 482 calories (22% calories from fat), 23 g protein, 75 g carbohydrates, 12 g total fat (2 g saturated fat), 0 mg cholesterol, 223 mg sodium

Italian Garden Pasta

Preparation time: About 25 minutes
Cooking time: About 15 minutes

●

Roma tomatoes, mushrooms, and plenty of leafy chard go into this fresh and hearty supper dish. For the pasta, choose the whimsical little corkscrews called *rotini*, or opt for elbow macaroni or another favorite shape.

12 ounces (340 g) Swiss chard

 1 pound (455 g) dried rotini or elbow macaroni

 3 tablespoons (45 ml) olive oil or salad oil

 1 pound (455 g) mushrooms, sliced

 1 medium-size onion, chopped

 3 cloves garlic, minced or pressed

 ½ cup (120 ml) canned vegetable broth

 ½ cup (43 g) grated Parmesan cheese

1½ pounds (680 g) pear-shaped (Roma-type) tomatoes, chopped and drained well

Trim and discard discolored stem ends from chard; then rinse and drain chard. Cut stems from leaves; finely chop stems and leaves, keeping them in separate piles.

In a 6- to 8-quart (6- to 8-liter) pan, cook rotini in about 4 quarts (3.8 liters) boiling water until just tender to bite (8 to 10 minutes); or cook according to package directions. Drain well, transfer to a warm wide bowl, and keep warm.

While pasta is cooking, heat oil in a wide nonstick frying pan or wok over medium-high heat. When oil is hot, add chard stems, mushrooms, onion, and garlic. Cover and cook until mushrooms release their liquid and onion is soft (about 6 minutes). Then uncover and stir-fry until liquid has evaporated and mushrooms are tinged with brown. Add broth and chard leaves; stir until chard is just wilted (1 to 2 more minutes).

Pour chard-mushroom mixture over pasta, sprinkle with half the cheese, and top with tomatoes. Mix gently but thoroughly. Sprinkle with remaining cheese. Makes 4 to 6 servings.

Per serving: 531 calories (22% calories from fat), 21 g protein, 84 g carbohydrates, 13 g total fat (3 g saturated fat), 8 mg cholesterol, 402 mg sodium

Vegetable Scramble Pockets

Preparation time: About 10 minutes
Cooking time: About 15 minutes

•

For breakfast, lunch, or supper, try these warm and filling sandwiches. Pita breads overflow with a colorful scramble of eggs, fresh vegetables, and feta cheese.

- 1 **large egg**
- 6 **large egg whites**
- 1 **teaspoon ground oregano**
- 1 **cup (about 4½ oz./130 g) crumbled feta cheese**
- 1 **tablespoon (15 ml) olive oil**
- 1 **large onion, thinly sliced**
- 2 **large red bell peppers (about 1 lb./455 g *total*), seeded and thinly sliced**
- 8 **ounces (230 g) mushrooms, thinly sliced**
- 1 **package (about 10 oz./285 g) frozen chopped spinach, thawed and squeezed dry**
  Pepper
- 4 **whole wheat pita breads (*each* about 6 inches/15 cm in diameter), cut crosswise into halves**

In a large bowl, lightly beat whole egg, egg whites, oregano, and cheese until blended. Set aside.

Heat oil in a wide nonstick frying pan or wok over medium-high heat. When oil is hot, add onion, bell peppers, and mushrooms; stir-fry until liquid has evaporated and mushrooms are tinged with brown (about 7 minutes). Add spinach to pan and stir-fry until heated through (about 3 minutes).

Pour egg mixture over vegetables in pan; stir-fry until eggs are softly set and look scrambled (3 to 5 minutes). Season to taste with pepper. Fill pita halves equally with egg mixture. Makes 4 servings.

Per serving: 398 calories (28% calories from fat), 22 g protein, 54 g carbohydrates, 13 g total fat (5 g saturated fat), 78 mg cholesterol, 813 mg sodium

Egg, Bean & Potato Hash

Preparation time: About 10 minutes
Cooking time: About 35 minutes

•

Great at any time of day, this mild hash of diced potatoes and red kidney beans is topped with gently cooked eggs. You can serve it straight out of the cooking pan—there's no need for a serving bowl.

- 1 **tablespoon butter or margarine**
- 1 **pound (455 g) small thin-skinned potatoes, scrubbed and cut into ¼-inch (6-mm) cubes**
- 1 **small red onion, cut into thin slivers**
- 1 **teaspoon chili powder**
- 1 **can (about 15 oz./430 g) red kidney beans, drained and rinsed**
- 1 **large tomato (about 8 oz./230 g), chopped**
- ¾ **teaspoon chopped fresh sage or ¼ teaspoon dried rubbed sage, or to taste**
- 4 **large eggs**
- ⅓ **cup (15 g) lightly packed cilantro leaves**
- ¾ **cup (180 ml) nonfat sour cream**

Melt butter in a wide nonstick frying pan or wok over medium-high heat. Add potatoes, onion, chili powder, and ¼ cup (60 ml) water. Stir-fry until potatoes are tinged with brown and tender when pierced (about 15 minutes; do not scorch). Add water, 1 tablespoon (15 ml) at a time, if pan appears dry.

Add beans, tomato, sage, and 2 tablespoons (30 ml) water to pan. Stir-fry gently until heated through, scraping any browned bits free from pan bottom. With a spoon, make 4 depressions in potato mixture; carefully break an egg into each depression. Reduce heat to low, cover, and cook until egg yolks are set to your liking

Continued on next page

Egg, Bean & Potato Hash (continued)

(about 15 minutes for firm but moist yolks). Sprinkle with cilantro and top with sour cream. Makes 4 servings.

Per serving: 328 calories (25% calories from fat), 18 g protein, 43 g carbohydrates, 9 g total fat (3 g saturated fat), 220 mg cholesterol, 280 mg sodium

---

Green Potatoes with Blue Cheese

Pictured on facing page
Preparation time: About 25 minutes
Cooking time: About 15 minutes

•

Here's an unusual main dish. Sautéed sliced potatoes are tossed with slivered fresh spinach and cilantro, then topped with a cool, zesty sauce of tofu and blue cheese. When you prepare and measure the spinach, reserve the best-looking leaves for lining the platter; use any torn ones for shredding.

Blue Cheese Sauce (recipe follows)

3 to 4 cups (3 to 4 oz./85 to 115 g) lightly packed rinsed, crisped spinach leaves

1 tablespoon butter or margarine

1¼ pounds (565 g) small red thin-skinned potatoes, scrubbed and cut crosswise into ¼-inch (6-mm) slices

1 medium-size red bell pepper (about 6 oz./170 g), seeded and cut into thin strips

1 medium-size onion, cut into thin slivers

1 tablespoon ground cumin

1 teaspoon ground coriander

¼ teaspoon salt

⅛ teaspoon ground red pepper (cayenne)

½ to ¾ cup (20 to 30 g) lightly packed cilantro leaves

Cilantro sprigs (optional)

Prepare Blue Cheese Sauce and set aside.

Cut 1 to 1½ cups (30 to 43 g) of the spinach into thin shreds about 2 inches (5 cm) long. Cover and set aside. Line a rimmed platter with remaining spinach leaves; cover and set aside.

Melt butter in a wide nonstick frying pan or wok over medium-high heat. Add potatoes, bell pepper, onion, cumin, coriander, salt, ground red pepper, and ¼ cup (60 ml) water. Stir-fry gently until potatoes are tinged with brown and tender when pierced (about 15 minutes; do not scorch). Add water, 1 tablespoon (15 ml) at a time, if pan appears dry.

Remove pan from heat. Sprinkle potato mixture with shredded spinach; mix gently but thoroughly. Then spoon potato mixture over spinach leaves on platter. Sprinkle with cilantro leaves; garnish with cilantro sprigs, if desired. Offer Blue Cheese Sauce to add to taste. Makes 4 servings.

Blue Cheese Sauce. In a blender or food processor, combine 4 ounces (115 g) **soft tofu,** rinsed and drained; ⅓ cup (80 ml) **low-fat buttermilk;** 1 tablespoon (15 ml) *each* **white wine vinegar** and **honey;** 1 teaspoon **Dijon mustard;** and 1 or 2 cloves **garlic** (peeled). Whirl until smoothly puréed. Gently mix in ½ cup (70 g) crumbled **blue-veined cheese.** Season to taste with **salt** and **pepper.** (At this point, you may cover and refrigerate for up to 3 hours.) Just before serving, stir in 1 tablespoon thinly sliced **green onion.**

Per serving: 279 calories (30% calories from fat), 11 g protein, 39 g carbohydrates, 9 g total fat (5 g saturated fat), 21 mg cholesterol, 436 mg sodium

---

Savory butter-sautéed potato slices and a peppery tofu-cheese sauce add up to Green Potatoes with Blue Cheese (recipe at left), a good-looking supper dish for any time of year.

Stir-fried Desserts

Stir-fried desserts? Why not? As these four recipes show, stir-frying is a great way to make warm fruit treats in minutes. Choose fresh pineapple chunks accented with lime and topped with crushed gingersnaps, or try a brandy-spiked combination of apples and dried cherries served with vanilla frozen yogurt. If you're looking for the perfect home-style treat, offer bowls of Sautéed Pear Crisp. And for a truly luscious dessert, top slices of pound cake with gently warmed banana slices and spoonfuls of rich chocolate-rum sauce.

Stir-fried Pineapple with Ginger

Preparation time: About 5 minutes
Cooking time: About 5 minutes

•

1 tablespoon butter or margarine

5 cups (775 g) ½-inch (1-cm) chunks fresh or canned pineapple

⅓ cup (70 g) firmly packed brown sugar

1 tablespoon finely chopped crystallized ginger

¼ teaspoon grated lime peel

1 tablespoon (15 ml) lime juice

1⅓ cups (100 g) coarsely crushed gingersnaps (about twelve 2-inch/5-cm cookies)

Mint sprigs

Melt butter in a wide nonstick frying pan or wok over medium-high heat.

Add pineapple, sugar, ginger, lime peel, and lime juice. Stir-fry gently until pineapple is heated through (about 5 minutes). Transfer fruit and sauce to a shallow serving bowl; sprinkle with crushed gingersnaps. Garnish with mint sprigs. Makes 4 servings.

Per serving: 291 calories (17% calories from fat), 2 g protein, 62 g carbohydrates, 6 g total fat (2 g saturated fat), 8 mg cholesterol, 178 mg sodium

Cherry & Apple Jubilee

Preparation time: About 10 minutes
Cooking time: About 7 minutes

•

½ cup (75 g) dried pitted cherries or raisins

2 tablespoons (30 ml) brandy

About 1 tablespoon (15 ml) kirsch

3 large Golden Delicious apples (about 1½ lbs./680 g *total*)

1 tablespoon (15 ml) lemon juice

⅓ cup (70 g) firmly packed brown sugar

2 cups (266 g) vanilla nonfat frozen yogurt

Mint sprigs

In a small bowl, combine cherries, brandy, and 1 tablespoon (15 ml) of the kirsch; let stand until cherries are softened (about 10 minutes), stirring occasionally.

Meanwhile, peel and core apples; then cut into ¼- to ½-inch-thick (6-mm- to 1-cm-thick) slices. Place in a large bowl, add lemon juice, and mix gently to coat. Set aside.

In a wide nonstick frying pan or wok, combine sugar and 2 tablespoons (30 ml) water. Add apples; stir-fry gently over medium-high heat until apples are almost tender when pierced (4 to 5 minutes). Add cherries (and any soaking liquid) and stir just until heated through.

Divide fruit mixture among 4 individual bowls; top equally with frozen yogurt. Garnish with mint sprigs. Offer additional kirsch to drizzle over yogurt, if desired. Makes 4 servings.

Per serving: 323 calories (1% calories from fat), 2 g protein, 74 g carbohydrates, 0.5 g total fat (0.1 g saturated fat), 0 mg cholesterol, 53 mg sodium

Sautéed Pear Crisp

Pictured on page 94
Preparation time: About 20 minutes
Cooking time: About 15 minutes

•

Crisp Topping (recipe follows)

½ cup (75 g) dried cranberries or raisins

3 tablespoons (45 ml) berry liqueur

4 large firm-ripe pears (about 2 lbs./905 g *total*)

4 teaspoons lemon juice

1 teaspoon butter or margarine

⅓ cup (70 g) firmly packed brown sugar

Vanilla nonfat frozen yogurt (optional)

Prepare Crisp Topping and set aside.

In a small bowl, combine cranberries and liqueur; then let stand until cranberries are softened (about 10 minutes), stirring occasionally. Meanwhile, peel, core, and thinly slice pears. Place in a large bowl, add lemon juice, and mix gently to coat; set aside.

Melt butter in a wide nonstick frying pan or wok over medium-high heat. Add sugar and pears. Stir-fry gently until pears are almost tender when pierced (about 4 minutes). Add cranberries (and any soaking liquid) and stir just until heated through.

With a slotted spoon, transfer fruit mixture to 4 individual bowls. Strain pan juices, if desired; then pour into a small pitcher. Sprinkle fruit with Crisp Topping. Top with frozen yogurt, if desired. Drizzle with pan juices. Makes 4 servings.

Crisp Topping. In a food processor or medium-size bowl, whirl or stir together ¾ cup (95 g) **all-purpose flour,** ⅓ cup (30 g) **regular rolled oats,** 3 tablespoons **sugar,** and 1 teaspoon **ground cinnamon.** Add ⅓ cup (76 g) firm **butter** or margarine (cut into chunks) and 1 to 2 teaspoons **water;** whirl or rub with your fingers until mixture is crumbly.

Press oat mixture into ½-inch (1-cm) chunks (some smaller chunks

and crumbs are fine, too). Transfer oat chunks to a wide nonstick frying pan or wok. Stir-fry gently over medium-high heat until golden (about 8 minutes; do not scorch). As you stir, gently scrape free any browned bits that stick to pan. Remove from pan. If made ahead, let cool completely; then cover airtight and store at room temperature for up to 2 days.

Per serving: 559 calories (28% calories from fat), 4 g protein, 96 g carbohydrates, 18 g total fat (10 g saturated fat), 44 mg cholesterol, 173 mg sodium

Bananas with Pound Cake & Chocolate Sauce

Preparation time: About 15 minutes
Cooking time: About 10 minutes

•

Chocolate-Rum Sauce (recipe follows)

3 large bananas (about 1½ lbs./680 g *total*)

1 tablespoon (15 ml) lemon juice

1 tablespoon sweetened shredded coconut

3 tablespoons granulated sugar

4 slices purchased nonfat pound cake (or use home-made or purchased regular pound cake), *each* about ¾ inch/2 cm thick

Prepare Chocolate-Rum Sauce; keep warm. Cut bananas into ½-inch (1-cm) slanting slices; place in a large bowl, add lemon juice, and mix gently to coat. Set aside.

In a wide nonstick frying pan or

wok, stir coconut over medium heat until golden (about 3 minutes). Remove from pan and set aside. To pan, add sugar and 2 tablespoons (30 ml) water. Cook over medium-high heat, stirring, until sugar is dissolved. Add bananas; stir-fry gently until bananas are hot and sauce is thick and bubbly (about 2 minutes). Remove from heat.

Place one slice of cake on each of 4 individual plates; spoon banana mixture over cake, drizzle with Chocolate-Rum Sauce, and sprinkle with coconut. Makes 4 servings.

Chocolate-Rum Sauce. In a small pan, combine ½ cup (110 g) firmly packed **brown sugar,** ¼ cup (20 g) **unsweetened cocoa,** 1 tablespoon **cornstarch,** and ¼ teaspoon **instant coffee powder.** Stir well. Add ½ cup (120 ml) **water** and 2 tablespoons (30 ml) **light corn syrup;** stir until smooth. Cook over medium-high heat, stirring constantly, until mixture boils and thickens slightly (about 4 minutes). At this point, you may cover (to prevent a film from forming on top), let cool, and refrigerate for up to 3 days. Reheat, stirring, before proceeding.

Remove pan from heat and stir in 2 teaspoons **light or dark rum** (or to taste) and ½ teaspoon **vanilla.** Keep warm, stirring occasionally. Just before serving, stir well.

Per serving: 410 calories (3% calories from fat), 4 g protein, 100 g carbohydrates, 2 g total fat (1 g saturated fat), 0 mg cholesterol, 225 mg sodium